DATING
BACKYARD DOGS

A GUIDE TO
CHRISTIAN DATING

BY LINN WINTERS

WESTBOW
PRESS®
A DIVISION OF THOMAS NELSON
& ZONDERVAN

WestBow Press books may be ordered through booksellers or by contacting:

WestBow Press
A Division of Thomas Nelson & Zondervan
1663 Liberty Drive
Bloomington, IN 47403
www.westbowpress.com
1 (866) 928-1240

Because of the dynamic nature of the Internet, any web addresses or
links contained in this book may have changed since publication and
may no longer be valid. The views expressed in this work are solely those
of the author and do not necessarily reflect the views of the publisher,
and the publisher hereby disclaims any responsibility for them.

Any people depicted in stock imagery provided by Thinkstock are models,
and such images are being used for illustrative purposes only.
Certain stock imagery © Thinkstock.

Scripture taken from the Holy Bible, NEW INTERNATIONAL VERSION®.
Copyright © 1973, 1978, 1984, 2011 by Biblica, Inc. All rights reserved worldwide.
Used by permission. NEW INTERNATIONAL VERSION® and NIV® are
registered trademarks of Biblica, Inc. Use of either trademark for the offering
of goods or services requires the prior written consent of Biblica US, Inc.

ISBN: 978-1-5127-5261-8 (sc)
ISBN: 978-1-5127-5262-5 (hc)
ISBN: 978-1-5127-5260-1 (e)

Library of Congress Control Number: 2016912866

Print information available on the last page.

WestBow Press rev. date: 8/31/2016

Introduction

You are probably wondering what a guy who hasn't dated in thirty-three years could possibly have to say about dating. It's a great question. Does it help to know that I was a serial dater? I had lots of experience in good relationships and some really bad ones. I watched the people I dated eventually go on and get married. Some of their marriages survived, while others failed miserably. Interestingly, I could have predicted many of those outcomes based on their behaviors while we were dating.

I also spent seventeen years in youth ministry. Believe me, I saw all kinds of dating; those who resolved to wait until marriage to have sex and those who didn't, couples who fought like cats and dogs, and others who seemingly never disagreed. I saw people who seemed to have nothing in common yet ended up in love, and those with everything in common who broke up. I was able to observe myriads of dating styles and tactics, and now years later it's easy to identify what worked and what didn't.

Maybe more importantly, I've been a Senior Pastor for the last twenty years and have counseled countless couples at the crossroads of their marriages only to learn that the seeds of their destruction were planted while they dated. Most married people problems are single people problems that they brought to the marriage. If it were possible to roll back time and equip them to make better choices about whom and how they dated, they could have avoided years of pain.

My heart is to share with you the experience a lifetime in ministry has brought me, to give you an advantage that others don't have, and to share what others wish they had known before they said, "I do."

Some reasons why you may want to consider reading this book:

- If you are in a relationship, and things just don't seem right.
- You are hoping the next relationship turns out better than the last.
- You know someone in an unhealthy relationship, and you're looking for a way to encourage him or her.

No matter your stage of life, I hope you will benefit from learning to identify backyard dogs and use this new knowledge to change your own dating habits and help others.

Contents

Choosing the Right Dog

1. The Problem with Backyard Dogs 1
2. The Myth of "The One" 11
3. Non-Negotiables 21
4. Settling for a Backyard Dog 27
5. Deciding to Become the One 37

Where Have All the Good Dogs Gone?

6. Where Have All The Good Men Gone?. 45
7. What a Woman Needs 53
8. What a Man Needs 63

Selfish Dogs

9. Backyard Love 73
10. Indoor Love 83

Indoor Dogs Who Date Outdoor Dogs

11. Leaving Jesus Out 107
12. The Yoke Principle. 113
13. Shaky Foundations 119
14. The Dog Bed 133
15. The Big Bed 147

16. Establishing Sexual Limits 157
17. Pulling a Joseph 167
18. The Non-Negotiables 175
19. Nine-Dollar Light Bulbs 183

Choosing the Right Dog

one

The Problem with Backyard Dogs

She pushed the door to her apartment open and tossed her mangled heap of keys onto the counter. They landed with a loud clanging sound like someone had dropped a tray of silverware. The sound bounced between the walls reminding her she had once again returned to an empty apartment. Tara pulled open the refrigerator to survey her dinner options. Everything looked the same. There were leftovers from dinner at her mom's on Sunday, but that was five days ago, and the container of chicken and rice was looking beyond soggy. The freezer was full of microwavable meals that all tasted eerily similar when cooked despite their labels promising robust flavors like Chicken Alfredo and three cheese pasta. Tara settled on Mandarin chicken from a frozen box she purchased several weeks ago at Wal-Mart. After two minutes and forty-five seconds, she nestled onto the couch to eat while watching Netflix.

It was amazing that with all those viewing options, there was nothing to watch. On the third time through the directory, Tara finally settled on a movie she had seen several years before but couldn't quite remember the details. Hopefully, it would be more memorable this time. Three hours later, she headed for bed. Teeth brushed and flossed. Make-up removed, and nighttime firming gel applied, she lay in bed waiting for sleep but sleep wouldn't come. The idea that watching television, eating, and working had become the total sum of her life haunted her. She spent her days getting up early, going to an administrative assistant job, daily talking to dozens of strangers on the phone who would forever remain strangers, and finally coming home to an empty apartment, warming up a precooked meal, and watching TV alone until she went to bed...alone. Then it occurred to her, an idea of such brilliance it would change everything; why had she not thought of it before? She drifted off to sleep thrilled with possibilities.

It was Saturday morning, and Tara had the entire day to put her new plan into action. Everything about the morning seemed brighter. Whipping up a smoothie for breakfast, she loaded the dishwasher and gave the apartment a quick cleaning in anticipation of later. She practically skipped out to her car. She had done her research; she knew exactly where she needed to go. The tires to her car melodically hummed along the pavement in a tone that sounded almost anxious. Was it possible that everything was coming into alignment, and her life would be forever different from this moment forward? Could everything really be taking a turn for the better?

Tara pulled into the animal shelter, strode through the doors, and marched straight up to the desk. She proudly announced that she was there to adopt a dog! The girl behind the desk smiled and informed her there was paperwork to fill out (multiple pages), and there would be a fee of one hundred and twenty seven dollars to cover spaying/neutering, de-worming medications, a tick and flea treatment, and the first year's licensing. This was not going to be as simple as anticipated Tara thought to herself. But a little paperwork never hurt anyone, and what was one hundred twenty seven dollars if her life became instantly more fulfilling?

Forty minutes later Tara was led to the back room. It was time to make her choice. This might be a little harder than she thought. How could she choose from the hundreds of dogs staring hopefully back at her? She walked down row after row of options. Kennels were everywhere, in some places the cages were even stacked one upon the other up to three high. There must have been more than one hundred dogs; how would she ever choose one?

As she came around the corner of what must have been the fifth row, she saw... him. He was absolutely adorable! Her heart was instantly smitten. "What's his name," she asked. "Let's see," the girl from the counter replied as she bent over to read a card affixed to the front of the cage. "Toby" she announced, and in that moment Tara knew.

Toby was an Australian Shepherd. "Aussies", as they are sometimes called, are extremely loyal to their owners. "They are actually working dogs and require lots of attention," the girl went on to say. "Do you have a large yard?" "No," said Tara, "just an apartment." "Then he will need lots of walks," she warned. That was ok; nothing was going to dissuade Tara now that she had found her "soul mate." Every minute it took to finalize the paperwork, hearing repeated warnings about dogs being lots of work and receiving countless pamphlets explaining how to care for a dog blurred together in an obscure drone. It was as if time was slogging through syrup, and she could do nothing to free herself from it.

Eventually, they were home. The evening could not have gone better! Toby followed Tara everywhere; it was as if they had an immediate, unbreakable bond. When she watched that evening's movie, he was right there snuggled up, chin in her lap. She would never need to feel alone again.

She laid in bed that night excited about her new life. The next morning she was up with the sun, and she couldn't wait to spend the entire day with Toby. Tara left her bedroom, rounded the corner to her living room, and walked into complete horror. The room looked like it had exploded. The cushions of her leather couch had been ripped open, and the foam lay shredded into thousands of tiny pieces strewn throughout the apartment. The wooden cross she purchased in Ecuador on a missions trip had been gnawed almost beyond recognition. The cross was relatively inexpensive, but the memories it held were irreplaceable, and now it lay debased. Expensive shoes were gnarled, the legs of two chairs revealed multiple teeth marks, four different pieces of decor lay in various states of destruction, her large banana plant toppled with dirt strewn all across the apartment floor, and to add insult to injury, there were several points of urination and one rather large solid donation in the center of the room.

Suddenly, the reality of her choice rudely barged into her comprehension. No matter how adorable Toby was, he possessed none of the self-control and discipline needed to live indoors...Toby was a backyard dog!

THE PROBLEM WITH BACKYARD DOGS

Like Tara, we all run the risk of inviting a backyard dog into our heart. What is a backyard dog? A backyard dog is someone who has decided they are the most important person in life; that their needs and expectations come ahead of everyone else's no matter the cost. They perpetually wrestle with God because He asks to be put first in their life. This is a problem for a backyard dog because they are determined to do what they want, when they want, and how they want. If someone struggles to put God first, the one who has loved them unconditionally, who has always had their best in mind, and who has never made a mistake will most definitely struggle to put the needs of another person ahead of their own.

Today's culture actually promotes a style of dating that breeds outdoor dogs. Society tells young adults to live "free" while you can. Have fun! Just be sure to use protection! It's as if we've created a responsibility free zone for anyone who is single - a kind of perpetual "Spring Break." "Because what happens in Vegas stays in Vegas." Singles are told to do whatever they want to do with whomever they want, and the more partners the better, because practice makes perfect, and all the fun will stop when they get married. It's ok to use one another for momentary pleasure, lie if necessary, and when it no longer works for you, break up and go off to find someone new. You can keep doing this over and over again with no

> The best predictor of future behavior is past behavior.

consequences till one day you decide it's time for a "serious relationship." Then you'll shift gears and start looking for "The One;" hopefully, someone who has not been too damaged from dating a string of backyard dogs.

This is the most destructive advice that could ever be given to a single adult. Why? It is because those actions are actually training up a backyard dog. Repeat behavior over and over again, and it will become a habit; repeat it for years, and it will become character. The best predictor of future behavior is past behavior, and the best predictor of how someone will behave in a marriage is how he or she behaved while dating. If someone you date has spent the last six or seven years behaving like an outdoor dog, why would you expect them to marry you and magically and instantaneously transform into an indoor dog?

Not too long after we had planted Cornerstone (the church I pastor), a new family joined the church. When you are small and just starting out, a family joining is a big deal. We were ecstatic. About two months later, his wife called me late one evening asking if I could help. She and her husband had been arguing. He was now out with friends at a bar falling down drunk, and the whole group was about to head over to a strip club. The wife wanted me to go drag him out of the bar and send him home before he engaged the strippers. So there I was, a young pastor of a new church, headed into a bar to argue a drunk into going home. The next day I met with him to find out what was going on. He revealed that he had been depressed because he had made some illegal business transactions that the government had recently uncovered. He was facing huge fines and probable bankruptcy.

About three weeks later, that same husband announced he wanted to start a men's ministry in our small church where he would advise other men how to lead their families. As graciously as I could, I thanked him for his offer and explained that in order to lead, he would have to establish a track record of leading his own home well. He was furious... how dare I turn down his offer. Our church had no men's ministry; he was offering to give us one. Whatever missteps he had made, they were in the past; remember it had been three weeks. Jesus had forgiven him, and we should too. I tried to explain there is a difference between forgiveness and credibility, and leading anything in the church required credibility. He left the church with a big stink, telling anyone who would listen how poorly I had treated him.

About six months later, a pastor from the church he and his family were attending called me. He informed me that he had been spending time with our mutual friend, and it was obvious I had offended him. I patiently and painstakingly walked him through the story. At the end, it was clear that the other pastor was giving equal veracity to his version of the story as he was to mine. He suggested that we meet to talk out our differences and offered that he would moderate. I declined. I knew that if we met, and his new pastor continued to give equal weight to both of our stories, nothing would be resolved. Instead, I offered this solution, let the man continue in his church for another six months, be sure to observe his behavior, and if after that time the pastor still felt a meeting was necessary, I would gladly make myself available.

About nine months later, I just happened to be attending a function with the other pastor. Afterward, I walked over and asked him if we still needed to have a meeting. His response, "Not a chance." The man's true colors had revealed themselves at the new church. Actually, I was disappointed. I was hoping he would have grown in his walk and would be making better choices. But, I wasn't surprised; experience teaches that... the best predictor of future behavior is past behavior!

> So ask yourself a question, "Why am I dating backyard dogs?"

So ask yourself a question, "Why am I dating backyard dogs?" If past behavior is the best predictor of future behavior what's going to change? If they've had bad relationships in the past, and you look at how they currently behave, what's your best guess as to what your future with them looks like? Isn't it naive to believe if one of you puts on a white dress and the other a black tux, a pastor says a few words over you, and mystically your outdoor dog will instantly transform into an indoor mate? Miraculously capable of navigating all the personal sacrifice, acts of kindness, and compromise required in a healthy marriage. The reason this never works is that marriage doesn't fix our problems; instead, it multiplies them. Many people get married believing marriage means they'll take whatever is the best in each of them and combine it to become an amazing couple. What they forget is that marriage also takes whatever is the worst in both of them to potentially create something very toxic.

What does this mean for you? You need to do whatever is necessary to avoid dating backyard dogs. Even if it means fewer dates, nights spent alone, and even risking making someone mad along the way. Whatever the cost, keep backyard dogs in the backyard! The surest way to end up with a backyard dog invited inside (your heart) is to date one. The problem with outdoor dogs is we fall in love with them. We begin to overlook their chewing and justify their potty mistakes. Even backyard dogs have real, genuine moments of goodness, moments when you feel like they actually care for you and would be willing to change. After a while you'll have so much time invested in your backyard dog you won't be able to face the idea of starting over with a new dog, so... you'll invite your backyard dog inside. Doesn't it make more sense to spend the remainder of your dating life dating the way God wants you to date, dating indoor dogs in order to set yourself up for success for the rest of your life?

In the next few chapters we'll discover how to identify backyard dogs, unpack the disappointment of settling for a backyard dog, and reveal the deepest needs of both men and women. Hopefully, you will decide that leaving Jesus out of your dating life is a major mistake. Ultimately learning to use valuable tools that will help you find your indoor dog. Join me for an exciting adventure that promises to change the rest of your life.

Questions

1. What are some behaviors of a backyard dog?

2. What draws people to date backyard dogs?

3. In a season of loneliness did you ever lower your dating standards?

4. Looking back on your dating history, did any of the people you dated have backyard tendencies?

   Which tendencies?

5. Based on what you've learned in this chapter, what will change in your life?

two

The Myth of "The One"

Movies and books are full of stories of people finding "The One." They create a very romantic picture of a mystical journey to find that perfect someone. They may sell a lot of books but they just aren't accurate, and can be dangerous. How many people have stayed in a relationship even after it became unhealthy thinking that there was no one else for them? They had located "The One" and now they needed to stay with "The One" despite the fact that the relationship had grown toxic.

Luke thought he had missed "The One." It was interesting because since missing out on "The One" Luke had dated some really amazing girls, and each time the relationship became serious, he would break it off. Finally, a friend sat Luke down and asked, "What's going on? You've dated a string of great girls and dumped every one of them when things got serious. What's the deal?"

Luke explained that years ago he dated a girl, Sara, from his hometown. From the moment he laid eyes on her he knew she was "The One." After weeks he had mustered the courage to ask her out. She was perfect in every way; she was strikingly beautiful, loved the Lord, and was a great kisser. They dated for three glorious weeks until he discovered she had been seeing someone behind his back, and they were now engaged. He was heartsick; he had missed his one. No girl he had dated since could measure up to her;

so, each time things got serious he started comparing his present relationship to Sara, and each time they fell short. He dumped girl after girl because they weren't Sara. He had come so close to the perfect girl, and he wasn't going to settle for anything less.

Here are the questions Luke's friend asked him next: Was Sara actually the perfect girl if she was the type of girl who would date someone else behind his back? If they had only dated for three weeks, how did he know she was perfect? Had he dated her long enough to actually uncover her flaws? Since he hadn't discovered her flaws, wasn't he holding her up as an unreal measurement of perfection that even if he were to date Sara again she would be unable to meet? Wouldn't it be healthier to stop holding all his dates up to some imaginary mark of perfection and let each girl stand on their own merit?

Luke didn't listen to the advice. He spent nearly twenty years dating girls, and dumping them for not being Sara. In his forties he began to panic, realizing he was likely to spend the rest of his life alone... he married the next girl he dated, and they divorced one year later.

> There isn't one perfect person for you. But, there is a perfect type of person for you.

Luke didn't take his friend's advice, but you can. There isn't one perfect person for you. But, there is a perfect type of person for you. So let's spend a little time dispelling myths about what you are actually looking for when you date and then focus in on the type of person you should date.

The Myth of Only One: The myth of "The One" only takes a few seconds to expose. Let's imagine for a moment that it were true. That God had set aside just one perfect individual for each one of us. This would actually be the cruelest thing God could do, because you and I would never end up with "The One." Here's why: Imagine there is a couple perfectly planned to meet each other by God. The girl in this scenario meets a boy who is not her "one" when she is sixteen. She doesn't possess the life experience to accurately assess that he is not her one. He on the other hand is drawn to her by lust. He doesn't care whether she is "The One" or not; he is acting on hormones. So they make a mistake, get pregnant, and decide to get married.

Now, what happens to the boy who was actually "The One" for her? What happens to the girl whom God planned for the guy who is now married? Nobody in the story can ever have "The One." Through no fault of their own two innocent people are doomed to be miserable. Eventually, they will marry, but of course it's the wrong one because their right one was unavailable. Now they have messed up even more lives because by marrying, they stole someone else's "One." Worse than all of that, what about the children born to these miss matched couples? Think about it; they should never have been born! And since they should never have been born, there has never been a "One" born for them. So, no matter whom they marry, they are messing up other people's lives, and their kids are really in a world of hurt. Now consider that the world has existed for well over two hundred generations of people marrying the wrong one and suddenly you realize that no one alive today should

13

have ever been born, and there are no "Ones" left for any of us! Which means no matter whom you marry, they are the "Wrong One." Clearly this isn't the way things work.

The "You Complete Me" Myth: It's a powerful moment in the movie Jerry Maguire. After stumbling and loosing the best relationship of his life because he thought he was settling for second best, Jerry comes to realize that his wife Dorothy, played by Renee Zellweger, is actually the right one for him because she makes up for all his shortcomings. Once coming to this revelation, he hurries home to Dorothy to try and win her back. He bursts into the living room, and there in front of a group of women holding an "I hate men" meeting, proclaims to Dorothy that he's ready to come home because, "You complete me."

Again, it may sell movie tickets but it is an incredibly unhealthy way to look for a spouse. The mistake is thinking you need to find someone who is good at the things you are bad at, and hopefully you will be good at the things they lack, and together you make a whole. At times this becomes your excuse for dating backyard dogs. The one you're dating may be really bad at holding down a job, but you are super dependable; so, together you'll be good. In reality you will more likely spend the rest of your lives fighting because the backyard dog still won't keep a job, and it will drive the "dependable" part of you crazy.

The problem is being good at something someone else is bad at doesn't fix them; it just provides lots of material for fights! If you are really impatient and you marry someone who is the master of patience, nothing bothers him or her.

Chances are you will constantly be irritated that nothing bothers them. You will perpetually ask why you're not making more progress on solving issues around the home, but the fact that the repairman hasn't shown up doesn't bother them like it bothers you, so they haven't called to see why he missed the appointment. If a husband is really good at saving and he marries a woman who is really adept at spending, they probably do not balance each other out; more likely, they are facing years of arguments about their finances (the number one cause of marital strife).

In actuality no person can complete you; only God can do that! It is disingenuous to come to a relationship with a philosophy of two halves making a whole. Because in reality it is a cop out, it takes you off the hook to work on yourself, to actually become a complete and whole person in Christ. It is unfair to ask someone else to be your perpetual crutch. If you are half a person, you're not ready to date, and you need to spend some time becoming the person God created you to be. Then and only then will you be ready for the healthy complete person God wants to bring you. Wouldn't it be unwise to come to a relationship as a needy half person? Relationship math is not addition; one half person plus one-half person does not equal one whole. Instead relationship math is multiplication, one half multiplied by one half equals one quarter of what you need for a healthy marriage. Take two uncooked incomplete people, throw them into a relationship together, and you

> In actuality, no person can complete you; only God can do that!

don't get a healthy whole, you get a diminished dysfunctional fraction. That's because relationships actually magnify our weaknesses. If you stop and think about it, I guarantee you've seen this over and over with your friends. She was needy and struggling, he was a little strange and stubborn, but once they stared dating, they're one huge hot mess! The world is full of marriages between people who looked for someone to complete or balance them but what they actually got was a lifetime of arguments and regret. It is so much healthier to look for someone who compliments you. This means that on the most important issues of life they actually see life from a similar perspective to you. This includes your view of God, how you handle money, how children should be raised, how to treat each other during a fight, the importance of family, etc. If those core beliefs are not deeply similar, you will forever be in conflict. Be sure that the areas you have differences in are secondary areas not core values. Then those differences will actually serve to compliment the relationship not incite conflict.

The search for a type: Dating is instead about finding a type, and although it may not seem as romantic as finding "The One" once you begin to look for a type, it opens up all sorts of possibilities for who you will spend the rest of your life with. It will also lead you to someone you can be deeply in love with for the rest of your life. This is because God, instead of saying you can only marry my choice for you, actually says, you need to marry a type of person, but beyond that marry the person you are most drawn to. This is a real relief for those of us who are worried that if it were left up to God, he'd choose a frumpy missionary nerd. Instead, God has only two requirements that anyone you date must meet (we'll get to those later in the book). By the way, those two requirements will exclude you from dating backyard dogs. Once someone meets God's big two, the rest is up to you! You can add whatever you want to the list as long as it's not in direct violation to God's Word.

In some ways, I treated my son Joshua's first car the way God treats our future spouse. I told Josh that I would help him buy his first car, but I had two requirements; it had to be economical (good gas mileage), and it had to be dependable (I didn't want it sitting in my driveway broken down all the time). Other than that, I didn't care what type of car he wanted. Josh called me a couple of weeks later and said, "Dad, I think I've found the car!" Guess what my first two questions were? Does it get good gas mileage? Is it dependable? To which he answered," Yes." Then he surprised me... he said, "Dad, it's red. Does that matter?" I was taken back; he had met my requirements, so I said, "No, I don't care if it's red." "Yeah but, I remember you said red cars fade in the Arizona sun," Josh countered. "They do," I replied "But that's up to you, my two requirements are met, and if you're okay with waxing that car constantly, if you like it enough to invest extra time into caring for it, that's your call."

That's exactly how God handles us. He has two non-negotiables that anyone you date must fulfill, but after that if you are willing to put up with snoring, or if you only want to date someone with brown hair and blue eyes, or if they need to be tall or short or have a great sense of humor, that's your call. You get to have huge input into your future spouse. How cool is that? This is actually really good news, because you and I never have to feel like we settled for second best. You simply fulfill God's requirements and then you get to decide the rest.

Questions

1. If there is just "one" person for you, what happens if they marry the wrong person?

2. What are some things you hope your mate won't want from you in a relationship?

3. What are some misconceptions people have about what the other person should provide in a relationship? (Financially, socially, physical pleasure, etc.)

4. What do you think God's two requirements are going to be for the person you date?

5. What are the things you lack, and how do you deal with it?

6. Based off what you read in this chapter, what will you do differently in choosing the people you date?

three

Non-Negotiables

I met Lisa my freshman year of Bible College in Texas. I had surrendered to ministry at the age of fifteen, and Bible College was the next logical step. So I jumped into my car two weeks before my eighteenth birthday and drove the thousand plus miles to Arlington, Texas. When I arrived I began to look for a church. My plan was to find a church that was frantic for volunteers. I was hoping that if they were needy enough they would let me serve in lots of ministries, and I would have the opportunity to gain tons of ministry experience. I found a desperate church, and I was soon leading the college and career class. So, there I was three months removed from high school myself teaching and leading a class in which I was the youngest member.

One day a stunningly beautiful girl walked into the class, and I was immediately smitten. The only problem was that she had walked in with another guy. He was a college freshman, and she was still a senior in high school and was attending with him. I watched the relationship for a while, and when it appeared to have cooled off, I made my move. The class was holding a masquerade party for the upcoming holiday, and I called Lisa to ask if she would be my date. She very kindly but promptly turned me down. That was all the hint I needed, and I moved on to greener pastures. About a year and a half later, a lady in the church, Jeannie, approached me and suggested that I ask Lisa out. I told her of my previously failed attempt, and Jeannie assured me that she had been talking to Lisa, that she was "dying" to go out with me, and that Lisa couldn't stop talking about me (something Lisa denies to this day, but I'm sticking with Jeannie's story). So, after church that day I approached Lisa in the parking lot and asked her out again. We dated two or three times, and it soon became apparent that Lisa was probably not Pastor's wife material. She was bartending and heavy into the club scene. She was dating a lot, and I mean a lot, of backyard dogs that were pretty far from God. If those were her type of guys, I knew I wasn't. The type of life I was offering would be very different from the one she was pursuing. I had some criteria for what I was looking for in a wife, and one was a passionate sold out follower of Jesus Christ. There was so little in common between us, that when I transferred colleges a few weeks later and moved away I didn't even think it was necessary to tell Lisa I was leaving.

Over the next year of Lisa's life a lot changed. She had rededicated her life to Christ. That same year, she was asked to be a counselor at high school camp. After one of the chapels, Lisa went forward to talk to the camp speaker. She told him how discouraged she was with her dating life. She had plenty of dates, but something was missing. His question to her was, "Do those guys love your Jesus the way you do, and if not, why are you dating them?" Lisa didn't have a good answer, she realized

> "Do those guys love your Jesus the way you do, and if not, why are you dating them?"

she was dating people simply because they had asked, and no one else had. The camp speaker then urged Lisa to consider her non-negotiables. What were the attributes she was looking for in a future husband? The next day she came back with a list of thirty-five attributes. After chuckling, he challenged her to narrow it to the top five and to write them down and carry them with her. That way the next time she was asked out on a date or saw someone she was potentially interested in she could refer to the card and know immediately if she should even consider dating them.

Lisa's top five:
Tall dark and handsome
Loves the Lord
Called to ministry
Responsible like my Dad
Spontaneous

It's interesting, because Lisa went from a serial dater to almost no dates. During the six months that followed only one guy met the non-negotiables. She dating him a few times, then decided there just wasn't enough spark, they found themselves in the dreaded "friend zone" and eventually stopped dating. All the while Lisa kept serving in the high school youth group and making huge strides in her walk with God.

One day my friend Owen who was still living in the Dallas Fort Worth area called me to ask if I would be the best man in his wedding. I agreed and during the phone conversation he mentioned that while I was there for the wedding I should look up Lisa. I told him about our two dates and that Lisa just wasn't headed the same direction as me; bottom line was she didn't meet my hopes for a future wife. Owen then filled me in on Lisa's transformation and thriving walk with Christ. This was highly intriguing to me because Lisa had met several of the conditions on my list, one of which was "smokin' hot."

When I landed in Dallas, Lisa met me at the airport. Instantly there was an amazing attraction. Since Owen and his fiancé were way behind on their wedding plans, Lisa and I spent the next few days together nonstop. It was like twenty dates all rolled into one (at least that's what I tell people). Somewhere in the whirlwind of planning, we both realized we had met each other's non-negotiables. So, after four days, I asked her to marry me. We just celebrated thirty-three years together, and Lisa is the most amazing pastor's wife I've ever met.

I'm not recommending four-day romances. Some things you do when you are young are just plain stupid. What I am recommending is a list of non-negotiables. I believe the reason Lisa and I were so deeply attracted to one another and why we had so much confidence in our decision was that we both had clearly defined what we were looking for in a lifetime partner. I thank God all the time for a camp speaker who challenged Lisa to write down her list and then stick to it. It changed my life, it changed her life, and it will change yours.

So here's my challenge to you. What are your non-negotiables? What are the top things you want in a spouse that you won't fudge on, not even a little. It's ok if your list starts out a little long like Lisa's. Over the next few chapters I'll help you whittle them down. In the end, God will want to reserve two non-negotiables for Himself, but the other three on the list are up to you. So dream away, are you thinking tall dark and handsome or exotic beauty? What will make you the happiest in a future mate? Is it blonde hair, a sense of humor, strong family values, or a good relationship with their parents? You decide and then begin to ask God to bring that type of person into your life. The exciting thing is as long as you keep first things first, as long as God gets to write the first two, He longs to give you the desires of your heart.

> "Delight yourself in the Lord and he will give
> you the desires of your heart." Psalms 37:4

He will actually join you in the hunt! Why not go big with your requirements? God is going to go big with His!

In the back of this book we've provided you with a page to fill out your own Non-negotiable List. My encouragement is that you take some time right now to start your list. Don't use the space in the book yet since your list will likely change. But start dreaming, and by the time you get to the end of this book deciding your five non-negotiables will be a snap.

four

Settling for a Backyard Dog

It is actually pretty common to experience dry spells in your dating. Often this leads to feelings of loneliness. In those times you may become frustrated with God. Why is He letting me feel lonely? Why hasn't He brought someone when all my friends seem to be dating? Has God short changed or forgotten you, or are you just not desirable to the opposite sex? What we miss is that often in the dry spells God is doing His best work to prepare you for a great person and a great Kingdom adventure. Dry spells and periods of loneliness teach us lessons that have the potential to make us highly attractive to the right person (we'll cover this in the next chapter). It's easy to get angry with God for allowing you to be alone, and you may decide to lend Him a helping hand. But, if you're not careful it is precisely in this season that you will settle for a backyard dog. Even though you know you shouldn't, you'll convince yourself you're dating them just for the time being. That if God had been better to you, you wouldn't need to resort to settling. When God finally gets His act together and brings you better prospects, you'll dump the backyard dog and move on to an indoor dog. The problem is, this almost never works. Once you settle for a backyard dog, you will almost always end up stuck with a backyard dog.

The number one problem with dating backyard dogs is they are lovable. Even if you try not to, it is likely that you

will fall in love with your backyard
dog. Ask every person who married
the wrong person, and it began with
a date. They will tell you, "I was
lonely, we went out, over time we
grew together, and I began to love my
backyard dog." But, even if you love

> Even if you
> love them...
> a backyard
> dog is still a
> backyard dog.

them... a backyard dog is still a backyard dog. Loving them
simply means you'll end up inviting their chaos and bad
behavior into your life for a lifetime. With every person
who ever settled for a backyard dog, most likely, somewhere
early in the relationship warning bells went off, something
said "this is not who you need in your life long term," but
they were lonely so they continued dating their backyard
dog, hoping for an indoor dog. Problem is, spend enough
time with a backyard dog, and you will be convinced you
can't live without them. You will stick with them no matter
what warnings your friends issue, or how many times God
nudges your heart about the relationship.

Rick had moved to California to serve an internship at
a church and finish studying for ministry at a local college.
Not long after he arrived it became apparent Rick was super
homesick. He walked everywhere with slumped shoulders
and a frown. Crazy thing was that school was going well,
and he was being really successful with the internship; he
had every reason to be excited. Instead, he couldn't shake a
sense of deep loneliness. Rather than wait on God, he went
looking for someone to solve his loneliness problem. He
found a girl attending his Bible College. He knew from the
beginning that she wasn't "The One", but he just wanted

someone...anyone. He was tired of being alone. Everything started out well enough. Soon the relationship began to move forward at breakneck speed. Before too long they were talking marriage. That's when her true colors came out. She was deeply insecure and resented any time Rick spent in ministry and not with her; she felt she should be the center of his universe. When they argued, their friends were appalled. Venomous words would spew from her lips. The other interns started calling her Linda (Blair) from the "Exorcist" movie. Probably not the kindest thing to say, but everyone expected her head to spin at any moment and green stuff to go flying from her mouth. Eventually Rick distanced himself from friends and his relationships at church because she caused such tension everywhere they went, and he felt compelled to defend her.

By the time his parents pleaded with him to reconsider their plans to marry, and despite the attempts of multiple friends to intervene, Rick wasn't able to hear any of it. He had fallen in love with his backyard dog. What had started out as Rick simply trying to fill his loneliness turned into a toxic relationship. Rick illustrates just how perilous dating a backyard dog can be.

Jake had dated a lot of girls off and on. Now he had decided it was time to get married. Oddly, his dating world had dried up. He decided to go on the hunt. He knew what he wanted, and it was time to find it. There just weren't many prospects. Then came Jody. From the beginning, friends tried to drop hints and questioned Jake as to what he saw in Jody. The answer was simple; she was the best thing currently available. Because Jake and Jody were an item, other girls who might have been interested in Jake looked elsewhere; they weren't going to break "girl code." Jody had always lived on the wild side, and her walk with God was nowhere near Jake's, but while they were dating she seemed content to "behave herself." Eventually Jake deemed he and Jody had dated "long enough." He knew she didn't possess some of the qualities of the person he had always imagined himself with, but he reasoned she was a good person, and he surely didn't want to go through the time and pain of breaking up and starting a new relationship from square one. Besides, he reasoned, "if he loved her enough, she would eventually come around." Jake settled for a backyard dog.

They were married and moved to a new state where they both found jobs. Unfortunately, their jobs required them to work opposite shifts. It didn't take long for the cracks in the marriage to show up. Jody began to go to clubs and stay out with friends. Jake reasoned it was just girls blowing off steam. Eventually things went cold in the relationship, and Jake decided that what they needed was a child, something to give them a common cause and to "re-focus" the relationship. Just a note, if the two adults in a relationship are acting like children, the last thing the relationship needs is another one. The pressure of a baby who needed constant care, and the added financial burdens a child brings, opposite schedules, and friends who gave really bad advice, caused Jody to eventually take off leaving Jake to raise their daughter. Bottom line, if you date backyard dogs, in all likelihood you'll end up with your backyard dog.

Another problem that arises when a committed Christian settles for someone who isn't living for God is that someone has to pretend. Either the person who isn't committed to God has to appear as if church and spiritual things are important to them or at least feign that they have a legitimate interest, or the committed Christ follower has to tone things down. Either way, one or both are pretending. Notice what the Bible says:

> "As iron sharpens iron, so one person sharpens another." Proverbs 27:17

The reverse principle is also true. It is possible for someone to dull your life. Some people are more like rocks than they are like iron. That type of individual will diminish God's plan and purpose for your life.

> "Do not be misled: "Bad company corrupts good character."" 1 Corinthians 15:33

It is highly unlikely for someone who hasn't settled on who God is in their own lives, whether they be: pre-Christian, baby Christian, or a backslidden Christian, to be a sharpening agent in your walk with Christ. If you're a Christian and you want to argue right now that the unsaved person you are dating is actually helping your relationship with God, the only way for that to be true is if you are incredibly young in the Lord. Get the tiniest bit of

> Decide to date someone living life far from your God, and you'll need to pretend that He isn't a priority to you either. Do that long enough and... you won't be pretending.

maturity, and you'll be well beyond anyone who doesn't know your Jesus. Decide to date someone living life far from your God, and you'll need to pretend that He isn't a priority to you either. Do that long enough and… you won't be pretending.

Perhaps the biggest mistake with dating someone just because they are convenient is that if an amazing person suddenly walks in the room they will assume you are taken. When single people enter a new group, they immediately begin to assess who is with whom. If you are in a relationship, even if it is with a person you are not serious about, the new person will relegate you to the unavailable pile. You will miss out on any opportunity to explore a potentially great relationship because you were involved with a convenient backyard dog. This can be catastrophic because a remarkable person, who is attracted to you and would have been interested, will look elsewhere because they see you dating Mr. or Miss right now. It is much wiser to keep yourself available. You do not win a prize for the most dates or for dating the longest. You win the prize by finding the right one for you, and you can't do that if the right one walks into the room and you're dating the wrong one. Better to be a little lonely during the dating process than to spend a lifetime wondering about the one who got away. Staying single and available keeps all your options open; settling for

> You win the prize by finding the right one for you, and you can't do that if the right one walks into the room and you're dating the wrong one.

Mr. or Miss right now takes you off the market, and if you haven't found the right one yet, you want to be on the market! This is why it is crucial that as soon as you realize the person you are dating is not a candidate for forever that you move on from that relationship. Loneliness is a bad reason to stay dating someone with whom you have no real future, and in a relationship that keeps the right ones from checking you out. Date the wrong one long enough, you'll begin to believe no one else is interested, and you'll settle for the one you're with.

Finally, your prospective dates will assume you are like the person you date. We have all seen people who were polar opposites dating. This is because it is not personality that draws us to the opposite sex; it is someone's character. Let any two individuals date, and it will be their shared values that determine if they stay together for any length of time. All of us have been initially attracted to someone only to discover after getting to really know him or her that the attraction was gone. This is because although physical attraction can ignite an initial spark, it is the character and personality of the individual that either fans or extinguishes the flames.

The simple truth is even if you're attracted to someone, if how they navigate life and choose to treat others is offensive to you, you will either walk away or decide to become like them. If you believe strongly in honesty, you will not continue to date a person who consistently lies. Their falsehoods will eventually drive you away. In the same way, if you date someone who holds a high value of being kind to others, and you are the type of individual who uses people for your own ends, chances are your relationship will be short lived.

Years ago I was leading a youth group outing. We had rented out the local bowling alley for two hours. The bowling alley was huge, and I would get a much better rate if we rented out the entire facility. So, we made an exception and mixed our high school group with our junior high kids. On the day of the event the parking lot was packed with kids. We loaded bus after bus with over 250 kids. On my bus, Eddie got on. Eddie was an outreach kid. One of the most obnoxious, rude, socially awkward young men I've ever met, and I'm being kind. By the time we drove the mere twenty minutes to the lanes, Eddie already had our entire bus ready to throw him off.

We unloaded at the lanes. Kids were left to pair up with friends on the lanes, but of course Eddie had no one to pair up with. I felt sorry for Eddie. I resolved that I would get us checked in and then hang out with Eddie so he wouldn't have to be alone. Fifteen minutes later, when I had finished the paperwork, I began my search for Eddie. Much to my amazement he was not alone. He had linked up with Adam, the most obnoxious, rude, socially awkward kid in junior high. It was astounding! How had they found each other in a room of hundreds so quickly? The answer is, character attracts.

We intuitively understand this principle. People who hang together over the long term must have common ground on the things that are important. It's why guys who know their friend is only interested in sex, then see him date a girl for any length of time, will naturally assume that the relationship must be physical. They inherently understand what the prophet Amos knew; that "two cannot walk together unless they agree." She may not have started out wanting a relationship based on sex, but you can't continue in a relationship with someone and not morph to the path.

If girls know their friend is deeply materialistic, they will assume her steady boyfriend probably does not have deep concern for the hungry or homeless. If he did, her relentless pursuit of stuff would grate on his social conscience. If he did care about the poor at all, that disagreement on core beliefs would have driven them apart.

All this translates into the reality that if in an attempt to not be lonely you settle for someone who has very different values from you, others who might have considered dating you will assume you share the values of the one you're dating. Fair or not, you will be judged by the company you keep!

Settling for your backyard dog is catastrophic. Chances are that all the indoor dogs will move on… and you'll be left with no options except your backyard dog. If you settle for dating Mr. or Miss right now, you will marry Mr. or Miss right now.

Questions

1. Why is it dangerous to even begin dating a backyard dog? How might it change you?

2. What are things people tell themselves that allows them to settle for "Mr./Miss Right Now"?

3. How do you protect yourself from getting into unhealthy relationships?

4. If you date a backyard dog, what will people assume about you?

5. What are your personal values? How could a future relationship support that?

6. How will this chapter affect your relationships?

five

Deciding to Become the One

Are you the one, the one you're looking for is looking for? What if the reason God has not brought the right person into your life is because you're not ready for them yet? What if God in His absolute kindness has not introduced them to you, because if they met you today they wouldn't recognize you? This really comes down to the simple question, "how cooked are you spiritually?"

If you were to ask God, am I the person you hoped I would be by now, how would He answer? If you have been resisting God and the growth He is trying to produce in your life, a byproduct of that rebellion may be that you aren't the person you need to be. He is unable to bring the person you're hoping for into your life because you wouldn't be ready for them, and they would push the "pass" button on you.

Is it possible you haven't met the one because you're not the one for them...yet? Perhaps they have progressed in their walk with God to a place further along than you have right now. If you were to be held up to their list of non-negotiables you would fail the criteria. What if God is still waiting for you to make the decisions that up until now you've put off. He knows that as soon as you do, as soon as you get serious about your Christian walk, you'll be ready to meet that someone special?

If you are finding yourself in a relational drought, the most important thing you can do is stop chasing a mate and focus on chasing after God. Be willing to ask Him if there are things you need to work on so that you'll be ready for the next relationship He has planned for you. It is also possible that the person you are supposed to date next has several decisions of their own to make, that if God brought them in the room now, you would be the one issuing a pass. What each of us needs to be willing to do is allow God the time to get them ready for us and us ready for them. If you decide to be patient you'll find there is real power in becoming The One".

> What each of us needs to be willing to do is allow God the time to get them ready for us and us ready for them.

When you allow God to do His work in you, it will come at a cost. Following God is never easy, actually it will be the hardest most courageous thing you do. I remember a time in high school when my Youth Pastor, Wayne, issued us a challenge to be a witness on our campuses. His challenge, carry our Bibles to class every day for a year. I knew exactly what that would mean. No more secret agent Christian for me. I knew there would be taunts, and possibly girls who I had been interested in would think I was too fanatical. But I felt deeply convicted that Wayne's challenge was something God wanted me to do. That it would force me to live out my faith publically and in spite of ridicule. So I began to carry my Bible every day to every class, and as you probably guessed I got teased and harassed... a lot. One day a member of our football team was spouting off before class. He was saying how Jesus was a crutch and only weaklings were Christians. My reply was "Oh yah, if you think it takes a weakling to follow Christ, you try carrying my Bible to class for a week." The thought of carrying my Bible around was so intimidating to him he never bothered me again. He realized it took courage to carry a Bible in a public school, and he wasn't up for the challenge. That moment is minor; following Christ has cost me a thousand fold, and I have the scars to prove it. Much like Paul who said:

> "I have worked much harder, been in prison more frequently, been flogged more severely, and been exposed to death again and again. Five times I received from the Jews the forty lashes minus one. Three times I was beaten with rods, once I was pelted with stones, three times I was shipwrecked, I spent a night and a day in the open sea, I have been constantly on the move. I have been in danger from rivers, in danger from bandits, in danger from my fellow Jews, in danger from the Gentiles; in danger in the city, in danger in the country, in danger at sea; and in danger from false believers. I have labored and toiled and have often gone without sleep; I have known hunger and thirst and have often gone without food; I have been cold and naked. Besides everything else, I face daily the pressure of my concern for all the churches." 2 Corinthians 11:23b-28

Certainly, I've experienced nothing near Paul's hardships; yet to follow Christ I have struggled financially, been falsely accused, deeply betrayed by friends, overlooked for promotion, fired, underpaid, surprisingly never overpaid, turned down for dates, lived in my mom's basement when I was 35 with my wife and child, and spent countless hours in a boys' cabin at camp (the smell alone can cause brain damage), but I wouldn't change a minute of it.

I guarantee you that if you decide to obediently follow Christ you will pay a price one hundred times over, you'll have battle scars from taking stands, from doing the right thing when others aren't, and from living differently than the crowd.

Here's the cool thing about deciding to pay the price to follow Jesus, it will help you recognize others with the same battle scars. If in your past you've been a person prone to lose their temper and to say hurtful things to others during a fight, then you know how big a deal it is to bring your tongue into subjection to Christ. I guarantee when you are around someone else who has every right to be irritated or retaliate verbally, and they have the spiritual maturity to hold their words, you will notice. If you've decided to honor God by the types of movies you attend, I promise you will take note when others choose to attend a show filled with sexual themes, nudity, or excessive language. You will also notice when others choose not to. When you begin to seriously pay the cost to follow Christ and honor him in every one of your decisions, you will begin to recognize others who have answered the same call and those who haven't. In other words becoming the right type of person will help you recognize the right type of person.

Take it from someone who knows, letting God make you the right person makes you really attractive to the right person. So let me ask again, are you the person, the person you're looking for is looking for?

Questions

1. Why do people have "dry spells" in dating?

2. Has the waiting on God ever proven to be worth it in your life?

3. Is there an area of your life that you know God has been nudging you to address? Areas to surrender? Truths to believe? Tendencies to work on?

4. How does becoming "the right one" help you recognize the right one?

5. Would you consider praying right now to give God permission to not bring the "right one" until you become the "right one"?

6. Based on this chapter, what do you need to do?

Where Have All the Good Dogs Gone?

SiX

Where Have All The Good Men Gone?

The cry of women in the church today is that you just can't find a good man. This is an interesting turn of events because in the early church, women flocked to the church because of the men they found there. It was the early church that for the first time in history began to value women. It was the way Jesus treated women, and the teachings of Paul that brought about a revolution. Imagine sitting as a male in the early church. The prevailing Roman culture of the day treated women as property. They ranked somewhere below a good set of oxen. Romans married and discarded wives as seasonally as they changed fashion. Men who could afford it had multiple mistresses on the side, and having sex outside marriage was considered normal. Sex with prostitutes and mistresses was actually considered a form of birth control so married men could avoid sex with their wives and the responsibility of a child.

In the midst of that prevailing culture Paul begins to teach that men are to love their wives:

> "Husbands, love your wives, just as Christ
> loved the church and gave himself up for her"
> Ephesians 5:25

Imagine how that went over in the first Bible study! Chances are some young man in the back timidly raised his hand, "are you saying that we are to love the girl?" Paul's reply, "Exactly." This would have been mind blowing to that generation! Up until now, they owned the girl, used the girl, and discarded the girl, but love the girl? Not a chance. And as if Paul had not pushed the envelope enough, "you are to lay down your life for her just as Christ laid down his life for the church." Again a hand rises at the back of the room, "Are you asking us to die for the girl?" "If need be", is Paul's reply. "You are to put her needs above your own needs, more important than dying for the girl, you are to live for her." "Treat her with care because she is the more delicate and precious vessel."

Although this was surely hard to swallow for men in the first century, when men began to catch on and practice what they had learned, women flocked to the church to find "real men." The church was the only source for the type of men women longed for. So how is it that Christian women today cannot find a good man in the church; why aren't women from outside the church still flocking to the church to find men who will treat them well? It's because modern culture has invaded our churches. Christian men treat women in the same disrespectful way as their secular counterparts. Christian men pressure women into sex. They treat them more like a product to be consumed rather than a sister in Christ. Christian men use the same language, spew the same hurtful words, and behave just as selfishly as any non-Christian. The problem is that when a man claims to be a follower of Christ yet acts no different than the world, a woman's disappointment is profoundly bigger, and it often leaves her spiritually disillusioned.

Truth be told, it's not just the church where it's hard to find a man. Our culture has cultivated a whole new breed of backyard dog, something not quite a boy but definitely not a man...we'll call them "guys". It's an interesting phenomenon. For thousands of years, males were boys, and then they were men. There were five rites of passage that marked the movement from boyhood to manhood, you finished training, left home, started your career, married, and had children. Often, these occurred in a very short period of time and often around the age of fourteen or fifteen.

Recently, society has created adolescence. Adolescence is unique to modern culture and represents a period of "teenage" years between boyhood and manhood. The adoption of adolescence is primarily a function of an emphasis on prolonged education. Until recently, the last 150 years or so, many people did not go to high school let alone college, but with modern culture it is not only normal but expected. Adolescence is probably not a bad thing in and of itself. Life today is vastly more complicated than in the past, and a prolonged period to maturity is probably appropriate.

The problem is that in this generation we've created a whole new category. Men and women are putting off getting married, and often not leaving home until they are well into their thirties. This is especially epidemic amongst males. They live with their parents or get an apartment with eight guys sleeping on mattresses on the floor so they have minimal rent, they speed through college on the nine-year plan, or they hold down part time jobs driving pizza delivery so they can spend as many hours as possible playing video games.

There may not be anything particularly sinful about living this way. I can't show you chapter and verse. But just because something is not sinful doesn't mean it's not stupid! I can eat dirt; it may not be sinful, but it qualifies as stupid. So does living like a twelve year old when you're thirty. I would also suggest that there is a certain amount of selfishness involved. To live into your thirties doing the bare minimum in life so that you can devote the maximum number of hours to defeating the "Orc kingdom" all the while contributing nothing to society, or world hunger, or investing in the next generation, or contributing to the lives of others around you is ultimately selfish and lazy. The lie is that somehow this is now "normal." There is nothing normal about it. And although in today's culture females are also taking a protracted adolescence they are tending to snap out of it at an earlier age, and when they do they begin to look around for a man, all they find are pizza delivery "guys". A recent development in our culture is women purposefully having children outside of marriage because they cannot find a mature male willing share the responsibilities of parenting.

> How convicting is it that today we cannot navigate the same life challenges that were previously navigated by fifteen year olds?

So, rather than take a guy into her home and having to raise two children at once, they are opting to parent on their own. How convicting is it that today we cannot navigate the same life challenges that were previously navigated by fifteen year olds?

One of the main attributes of "guys" is a desire to avoid responsibility at all costs. Their mantra is, "what's the least I can do while having the most fun." At first glance this might seem like a desirable outlook on life. The problem is that in avoiding responsibility, "guys" are actually avoiding the very things God designed them to do - to work, to contribute to make society and the world better because they lived, to care for and protect their wife, to raise the next generation to be better than themselves, and most importantly, to discover what God created them to accomplish on this earth. Satan must be rolling in laughter. He no longer has to struggle to derail Christian men; they are too busy sitting on the couch playing Xbox and watching porn. I have nothing against video games, I am actually a gamer myself; video games just can't become the total sum of your accomplishment on this earth. Guys will never know the satisfaction of doing what they were created to do and hearing God say well done good and faithful servant. They will simply spend their lives as boys who shave. If you lay around all the time doing close to nothing and getting up off the couch only to eat and relieve yourself, how are you different from my neighbor's backyard dog besides the fact that he barks?

They will simply spend their lives as boys who shave.

Our culture reinforces this notion that males don't need to accomplish or take responsibility for anything. Instead they tell guys, drink our beer and you'll be a man. Buy our truck because real men buy trucks. Play our video game, save the cyber damsel, and you will have achieved significance. Sleep with every vulnerable girl looking for love. Leave a trail of broken hearts and souls, and you'll be a man! Do not believe those lies. There is nothing you can consume, no vehicle you can buy, and no

> Manhood is not something you consume; it is something you become when you take your God given place in this world.

number of sexual encounters that will make you a man. Manhood is not something you consume; it is something you become when you take your God given place in this world.

Perhaps the insidious form of the backyard dog is the "guy," males old enough to be men but living like boys. This generation will have to decide if they are going to become selfish consumers or strive to live up to the hope God has placed in them. I'm convinced that the best men anywhere ought to be in the church. If you and I claim to be followers of Christ, then the words of Paul are just as true today. We should treat women with such high regard that the church would have the reputation that "The best place to find a man is in the church." How cool would it be if women once again flocked to the church because it was where you find real men?

Questions

1. What defines a "guy" as opposed to a "man?"

Guy	Man
_____	_____
_____	_____
_____	_____
_____	_____
_____	_____

2. Why is it dangerous for a woman to date a guy?

3. Why is embracing responsibility critical?

4. Why is it easier if manhood were something to consume rather than become?

5. Based on this chapter, what will change in your life?

seven

What a Woman Needs

When a man dates a woman, he is auditioning to be her man. He is saying to her, "from the time you were a little girl you have been waiting for 'The Man'...I'm him!" In the end, what she is hoping for is a provider. Men get this wrong because they believe this is entirely a financial request. Men come home from work believing they have done everything their wife needs from them. Nothing could be further from the truth. Women not only need financial stability, but emotional connection, spiritual leadership, and an exclusive commitment. This is why no woman should ever date a "guy." This new breed, backyard guys, who refuse to grow up and be men are by very definition incapable of providing what a woman longs for. A man may accidently neglect his responsibilities, but a backyard guy does not even posses the necessary abilities to fulfill her heart. This becomes clear when you compare what women need and how backyard guys behave.

Women need men who provide financially. Women, by God's design, long for security, this is why women nest. The moment they marry, they begin putting together their home. In a woman's heart she is providing a safe and secure place for her family. She hopes her husband will do the same. When he provides financially, he provides a secure environment. The bills are covered; the family's basic needs are met. This is a God given role for a man; scripture says that any man who does not provide for his family is worse than an infidel.

> "Anyone who does not provide for their relatives, and especially for their own household, has denied the faith and is worse than an unbeliever." 1 Timothy 5:8

This does not mean that he has to earn more than his wife; it simply means that the family's financial security is his responsibility. For the first twenty-six years of our marriage Lisa had a higher income than I did. I'm in ministry; I spent seventeen years as a youth pastor. If you know anything about ministry salaries then you know she didn't have to earn a lot to earn more than me. Despite the fact that she earned the majority of our family's income, it has always been my responsibility to ensure that our family was secure. At one point I found myself between ministry jobs. Despite my best efforts I could not find a church needing my services. After a couple of months, I knew we needed my income, so I started mowing lawns. It was Arizona in the summer, 115 degrees plus, and an average of eight to ten yards a day. It's what you do when your family needs you. There wasn't anything glamorous about it. It was hard work and a little humiliating to have graduated college only to be reduced to a job I had done as a ten year old. Men who understand the power of providing will do whatever it takes.

Backyard "Guys" don't have careers; they have hobbies. That's why they work as little as possible to earn the bare minimum so they can spend their free time watching porn, playing in a band, gambling online, or doing research for their fantasy football league.

Men are to provide protection: Protection is both physical and emotional. It's why God created him stronger than her. Ladies don't get freaked out by this; it simply means he can beat you at wrestling. If he can't... why are you dating him? Why do men open doors for women? She has arms! It's because his gesture communicates, "My strength is intended for your blessing." It is a sign that he will leverage his strength to protect her and never to harm her. This wiring on her part by God to receive protection from him is why it is such a violation when a man lifts his hand against a woman. It violates his manhood and her womanhood. It is an equally deep violation when he harms her with the strength of his words. Which is why men... I don't care what she said, it doesn't matter which button she just pushed, despite how disrespectful she may have been... you never use your words to harm her! You're the man, so in that moment be a man. Your strength is always to be leveraged for her protection and never for her harm.

When I was five, I was walking home from church with my grandma. Suddenly she stopped and said, "Linn, you are walking on the wrong side of the sidewalk. You're supposed to be on the side closest to the street so that if a car comes by and splashes you will take the water for me. More importantly, if a car comes careening down the road and is about to hit us, you can push me out of the way even if the car still hits you."

Now, I was only five at the time. Truthfully my grandma was much stronger and more capable than me. But, you get what she was doing… she was calling a five year-old boy to become a man. I walked the remainder of the way home on high alert, carefully studying every car as it passed. I was hoping some wild driver would loose control, and I would have the opportunity to "save the girl". God wrote, "protect the girl" on the heart of every man and "receive his strength" on the heart of every woman. It is one of *the* more powerful ways a man demonstrates love!

Men are to provide the spiritual tone and direction for their families. Interestingly, many men struggle to know how to provide spiritual leadership for their home. It is as easy as coming up with a basic business plan. The goal of every man should be that his wife and children would be better Christians because of his influence. So, if you want your children to grow up to be a better Christian than you, how often should your family go to church? Once you answer that question…if you do it, that's spiritual leadership! If you want them to be sold out for Christ when football practice conflicts with their discipleship group, which one should you encourage them to choose if you want them to be a better follower of Christ than you? How often should their father read Bible stories at bedtime? If you want your wife to grow significantly in

> The goal of every man should be that his wife and children would be better Christians because of his influence.

her walk this year, should you do more than simply attend Sunday services, or should you join a small group or attend a class at church as a couple? When you come up with a plan of what would move your family into a deeper love relationship with Jesus Christ, lead out into that plan; that's spiritual leadership.

A woman's heart yearns for her man to lead out in spiritual matters. This begins in the dating relationship. Every man should step forward to set the tone for the courtship as one that will honor God. He should set a clear direction that requires both of them to grow spiritually. Even if you don't eventually get married, your goal should be that every girl you date would be closer to God because she dated you.

> This makes it impossible for a backyard guy to take spiritual leadership in the relationship, often being dragged along by the girl he is dating because she is further along spiritually.

Backyard guys are adrift spiritually. They haven't figured out where God fits in their life or where they fit with Him. They may have affection for God but they do not love Him. When you truly love something it takes on a higher priority than your own selfish agenda. If guys truly loved God they would be seeking His will for their lives, not trying to avoid responsibility and maximize fun. Living for Christ is dying to self.

"I am crucified with Christ, Never the less
I live, yet not I but Christ lives in me, and

the life that I now live I live by the Son of God who loved me and gave himself for me." Galatians 2:20

This makes it impossible for a backyard guy to take spiritual leadership in the relationship, often being dragged along by the girl he is dating because she is more mature spiritually. All the while he is still stuck on the couch spiritually.

Fourth, she needs you to provide commitment. This again harkens back to the very core of what it means to be a woman. She is hoping to find the man who loves her more than anything else in the world. In a woman's world, this is expressed by commitment. This is why women are so interested in the "status" of the relationship. What she is really seeking to determine is the level of commitment and ultimately the level of love. For a woman commitment's importance not only means the relationship will last but also that she is held in first place in her man's heart. She has no desire to be with a man who has emotional mistresses.

Men inevitably get this wrong. Men by nature are task oriented. Because of this, the courtship can actually become a task to him, a challenge to win the girl. Because men are competitive, he does whatever it takes to win the game. He heaps attention on her and tries any number of ways to express his love for her. The problem comes after he wins. They get married,

> Women need a man who will provide commitment.

and without even realizing what he is doing, he checks off the task, "got the girl." He then moves on to the next task on his "to do" list. Sometimes this is finishing his education or pursuing a career. In the end, it doesn't matter what he moves on to, the problem is…he moved on. He has shifted his attention and pursuit away from her and onto something else. The chase has ceased! To the heart of a woman this is a profound betrayal. In her heart, commitment meant she would always be first, always be pursued. Suddenly, first for him is the next rung on the corporate ladder or going hunting. Everything that holds his attention more than his wife will feel like a rival to her because commitment to her is synonymous with first place in his heart.

Real men reserve the first place in their heart for their Lord and for their woman, nothing else is allowed to interfere.

Backyard dogs are unable to commit because they are not truly interested in the girl, but instead in what they can get from the girl. They won't commit because they want to keep their options open. If someone better comes along they want the freedom to jump the fence. In the mean time they have no problem using the girl they are with.

> Backyard dogs are unable to commit because they are not truly interested in the girl, but instead in what they can get from the girl.

I can hear backyard guys everywhere calling out in protest, "you've got us all wrong, we really do care about the girl, and we are not just using her for what we can get!" Prove me wrong…set down this book, walk into the other room…since you're probably living with her, get down on one knee and commit. I'll wait till you get back……….. Still here? I thought so. If you had gone to the next room, taken on the responsibility of her heart, and made a true commitment to her, that very act would have meant you weren't a backyard kind of guy in the first place or at least not one any more.

My question to every woman out there, why are you dating "guys"? You realize backyard "guys" are the worst form of backyard dogs. In actuality, they may be more like cats, looking for a place to sleep, eat, and poop but unless you're scratching their bellies, they are off to the neighbor's yard. You realize a backyard "guy" is incapable of ever meeting your needs because you need a man, not a boy with a razor. I don't understand why women keep coddling guys. I fully expect to see some twenty-six year old being pushed through the mall in a stroller by his girlfriend. He'll be holding a sippy cup filled with beer, have a beef jerky "binkey" in his mouth, and complaining his diaper is poopy while heading into Game Stop. I can anticipate the next words out of her mouth, "But I love him. He has so much potential." Let me assure you, that is not romantic love; it is actually your maternal instinct! It's the same thing you feel when you see a four year-old about to walk into the street, you want to rescue him. Ladies, if you settle for a "guy" you

> If you need a child in your life that badly let me encourage you to get yours the old fashioned way and not adopt a fully-grown one from his mom.

will never know the passion or fulfillment of being with a real man! If you need a child in your life that badly let me encourage you to get yours the old fashioned way and not adopt a fully-grown one from his mom.

Questions

1. What are the four things a woman needs from a man?

   A. _____

   B. _____

   C. _____

   D. _____

5. What do these look like lived out in a relationship?

6. Who are backyard dogs worried about providing for?

7. What does commitment mean to a woman?

8. Based on what you read in this chapter, what will you do differently?

eight

What a Man Needs

This may be the hardest chapter to grasp. That's because on first glance the backyard girl will appear to be giving the man exactly what he wants and needs. It's only with further investigation that we discover his backyard dog is duping him. So lets begin with a little Bible study. Ephesians 5:21-33 says:

> "Submit to one another out of reverence for Christ. Wives submit to your husbands as to the Lord. For the husband is the head of the wife as Christ is the head of the church, his body of which he is the Savior. Now as the church submits to Christ, so also wives should submit to their husbands in everything. Husbands love your wives, just as Christ loved the church and gave himself up for her to make her holy, cleansing her by the washing with water through the word, and to present her to himself as a radiant church, without stain or wrinkle or any other blemish, but holy and blameless. In the same way, husbands ought to love their wives as their bodies. He who loves his wife loves himself. After all, no one ever hated his own body, but feeds and cares for it, just as Christ does the church- for we are members of his

body. For this reason a man will leave his father and mother and be united to his wife, and the two will become one flesh. This is a profound mystery- but I am talking about Christ and the church. However each one of you must love his wife as he loves himself, and the wife must respect her husband."

You may be thinking, "How does this apply to dating? Ephesians 5 is all about marriage, and that's a long way off for me." Dating is an audition for marriage, and although you may be young now, and marriage is a long way off, what is essential during dating is that you are developing the skills that will help you identify the right mate capable of doing healthy marriage. The behaviors exhibited in dating will be exacerbated by marriage. She pouts now, she'll nag then, she is insecure now, she'll make you account for every minute then, she argues now, she'll throw tantrums then. You get the point. Marriage has a way of making molehills into mountains.

Lisa and I had dated a lot before we met. I'm convinced that those relationships prepared us to more accurately recognize each other when we finally went out for the first time. The passage in Ephesians is loaded with real life insights, but let's unpack just a few. Notice that the job descriptions for a husband and a wife are vastly different. The husband is to love his wife, but the wife is to submit and respect her husband.

Is it interesting that God did not command the wife to love her husband or the husband to respect his wife? This isn't an oversight, and it's not because the husbands doesn't need love or the wife doesn't deserve respect; it's because God knew how He wired men and women and what would be the most essential on a man or woman's priority list.

The reason He charges men to love their wives is because men tend to love in increments. Men are very hesitant to give their entire hearts to anyone, including God. Ironically, this is exactly what women long for, a man who will freely and without reservation give his heart. It is why so many wives are disillusioned after they marry their prince, and he runs off to attend to his mistress of career. Remember in the last chapter that we encouraged men to be providers for the financial, protection, spiritual, and commitment needs of a woman? This is because in order to actually accomplish this he will have to make her the highest priority in his life (outside of God).

So what is it that a man needs from a woman? Surprisingly, his highest needs don't involve love. This is not to say that love isn't important to a man, just that it's not number one or even number two. So what are the deepest needs of a male? Sex and respect are. This is where dating backyard girls can be super confusing for a male. More than likely, the backyard dog makes herself available to meet his sexual needs and indoor females don't. This may throw a man off track because he is thinking to himself, "this is a big deal in my life, and these backyard dogs seem to be much more in tune with what I need."

This is a huge danger zone for any male. First, the girl who is willing to have sex with him outside marriage is actually trying to steer and control the relationship toward her own goals, possibly marriage and commitment. Her goals aren't bad; it's how she's manipulating him to get them. When a male starts having sex with a female, he becomes instantly stupid! Sex is Novocain for the brain! His brain becomes so muddled; he no longer can accurately evaluate the relationship. You've heard of beer goggles; they are actually sex goggles. He will not see her shortcomings and faults in perspective. All he knows is he's getting what he wants. He lets the little head do the thinking his big head ought to be doing. I could tell you story after story where others and myself have tried to warn a friend that the person they were dating was the wrong one, that the relationship was obviously toxic. After submitting mountains of evidence, they still couldn't see it. It was clear to them that the person they were dating was perfect for them, and they had an excuse for every shortcoming. When someone is that oblivious, you can be assured, they are sleeping together!

Dating relationships that become sexual before marriage often end in disaster for the man. This is because his other core need, respect, is actually being deeply dishonored. Remember scripture commanded the wife to submit and respect. In actuality, the girl who will use sex in a relationship to get her way is doing just the opposite of that because she's actually manipulating him. She does not respect him or his leadership and sees him as someone to be maneuvered to her desires. She is utilizing sex to distract and control. The idea is "I'm willing to forge a connection with you that will keep you from considering other options" and actually gives her the upper hand in moving the relationship toward her desired destination. Don't be surprised when he doesn't behave the way she wants and withholding sex immediately becomes her weapon of choice to bring him back into subjection.

Using sexuality to manipulate a man is disrespectful. It is a clear statement on her part that if he were left to his own devices, he would fail to lead the relationship well. She does not trust or respect his leadership, so she leads him by exploiting his vulnerabilities. I'm not trying to make men victims here. I'm just encouraging them not to be stupid.

> Don't be surprised when he doesn't behave the way she wants and withholding sex immediately becomes her weapon of choice to bring him back into subjection.

"At the window of my house I looked down through the lattice. I saw among the simple, I noticed among the young men, a youth who had no sense. He was going down the street near her corner, walking along in the direction of her house at twilight, as the day was fading, as the dark of night set in. Then out came a woman to meet him, dressed like a prostitute and with crafty intent. (She is unruly and defiant, her feet never stay at home; now in the street, now in the squares, at every corner she lurks.) She took hold of him and kissed him and with a brazen face she said: "Today I fulfilled my vows, and I have food from my fellowship offering at home. So I came out to meet you; I looked for you and have found you! I have covered my bed with colored linens from Egypt. I have perfumed my bed with myrrh, aloes and cinnamon. Come, let's drink deeply of love till morning; let's enjoy ourselves with love! My husband is not at home; he has gone on a long journey. He took his purse filled with money and will not be home till full moon." With persuasive words she led him astray; she seduced him with her smooth talk. All at once he followed her like an ox going to the slaughter, like a deer stepping into a noose till an arrow pierces his liver, like a bird darting into a snare, little knowing it will cost him his life." Proverbs 7:6-23

Because a male can't get one of his core needs righteously met before marriage, he must focus on respect during dating. Does she give you honor as you lead in the relationship and make decisions? This doesn't mean she is a doormat. Wise men always take into consideration the heart and needs of their wife/girlfriend. Remember, his commission from God is to love her more than himself and put her needs above his own. Which means he'll be making a lot

Ladies, if you are the one doing all the giving in the relationship, he does not love you; you are simply convenient.

of adjustments and concessions because it blesses her heart, and when she sees him doing that, she'll know he loves her. Ladies, if you are the one doing all the giving in the relationship, he does not love you; you are simply convenient.

Men, there will be moments when after hearing input and taking her thoughts into full consideration you'll feel compelled to lead in a direction she doesn't understand. This will be a pivotal moment. The key is, in that moment, how does she respond? Respect isn't shown when you agree with someone. Respect's most beautiful expression occurs when you choose to follow despite the disagreement. Let me give you some powerful insight, if you have a woman who will respect you like that, and who trusts you fully, you won't have any problems in the sex department. She has already completely given herself to you emotionally. The physical side will be automatic for her. That's why God told you to start with her heart not her body. In the end, indoor girls are much better than outdoor dogs because they don't use one of a man's greatest needs, sex, as a weapon to disrespect and manipulate him.

Questions

1. What are the two core needs of a man?

   _____

   _____

2. How can a male become confused and believe that a backyard female is fulfilling his needs?

3. Why do you think some females use sex to manipulate males?

4. What is the one need a male should concentrate on while dating? Why?

5. What stood out in this chapter for you?

Selfish Dogs

nine

Backyard Love

Most of us hope to one day find "The One," that person with whom we were intended to spend the rest of our lives. Yet despite lots of effort and the best of intentions, around half the marriages in the United States end in divorce. Add to that the number of couples who stay together in unhappy marriages for the sake of the kids. The number of relational shipwrecks is staggering. How is it possible that so many who started out willing to do whatever it took to achieve a good marriage failed? The answer is that many of us are marrying our backyard dogs, and backyard dogs come to marriage with none of the necessary skills to be indoor dogs. They have spent their entire adult life doing what they wanted to do and selfishly using others. Being highly proficient at selfishness may serve you well on a reality television show, but it is disastrous in a committed relationship.

In Disney's "Lady and the Tramp," Lady, a well-mannered refined dog, meets Tramp, a reckless self-absorbed dog. Over time they find love, and Tramp is transformed into the dog Lady always dreamed he could be. The problem with that story is that it only happens in fairy tales. It's the old "kiss enough frogs and you'll find a prince" myth. Wouldn't it be more effective to spend your time kissing princes if you wanted to find a prince? The problem with marrying a backyard dog that has demonstrated selfishness throughout your dating life is that they can't simply turn selfishness off.

Ask any girl who has ever tried kissing frogs; they have a tendency to remain frogs, and backyard dogs tend to retain backyard behavior. Selfishness becomes a living part of a person's character, and with each selfish act they indulge in, selfishness digs its claws a little deeper into their souls. After a while it becomes hard to tell where their selfishness ends and they actually begin. It's as if selfishness is who they've become, and they would be lost without it. Their self-centered wants and desires will end up meaning more to them than any other person. They will spend their energy and attention focused on how to meet their own needs. Every other human will always come in a distant second.

By the time a backyard dog finds the person they were supposed to be with, they have spent so much time in the backyard, they are incapable of truly loving anyone else. They may try with the best of intentions, but it will always turn out to be a selfish kind of love.

Selfish love is when someone loves you primarily for what you do for them or because of how you make them feel (notice the focus here is on themselves). The opposite of selfish love is *selfless* love. Selfless love loves someone more than you love yourself and is willing to put his or her needs above your own; someone with whom you find your deepest joy in their happiness even if it means setting aside your own desires. Simply put, making them happy is what makes you happy.

In contrast backyard dogs love others "because" or "if." "Because" love loves others because of something they bring to the relationship. A girl may marry a guy because he has lots of money. When this happens, she actually loves him not for him, but for what he can purchase her. There is nothing real about that kind of love; it is simply selfishness dressed in nice clothes and new shoes. This is one reason guys intuitively recoil from women who are primarily interested in their net worth. Let the guy lose his job for an extended period or experience an injury and have to go on disability, and you'll soon see the shallowness of because of love.

Conversely, a guy may love a girl because she is beautiful. He knows all his friends admire him for snagging someone so good looking. He feels pride having her by his side and being able to call her "his," much like a possession. I'm not saying attraction isn't important; actually, it's huge. The last thing you would want is to be in a lifetime relationship with someone you are not attracted to. It just can't be the reason you love them! If the reason you love someone is because being with him or her raises your status or makes you look better to others then in actuality you love them because they serve your selfish desire to be admired. It's why selfish love is not love at all. Besides, no mater how good the person you are dating looks now, all that WILL change. Take it from someone who is…well, older than he used to be, and the jeans don't fit quite the same.

Just last night I was looking on social media and saw a friend's posting celebrating nineteen years since his wife had agreed to marry him. I've always wondered because she has always appeared to me to be way out of his league. Along with the posting was a picture of when they had

> Before you selfishly marry someone because they look good consider this, "Gravity always wins."

become engaged. Wow, was he different back then! My wife even commented, "Now I get why she said yes." But over nineteen years, things had changed. He had lots of health issues; gained over 100 pounds, and stress had created deep crevices in a once smooth youthful face. Before you selfishly marry someone "because" they look good consider this, "GRAVITY ALWAYS WINS."

Then there is the I love you "if" brand of love. I love you "if" occurs when your affection for someone depends on behavior or performance. I love you if you always agree with me or let me have my way. I love you if you will have sex with me. I love you if you pander to my insecurity and check in every hour. I love you "if" is the key factor in conditional love. The truth is "if" love isn't love at all, yet it is the most common expression of love between couples. The easiest way to expose I love you "if" is to consider the love of a parent for their child. From the moment their baby comes into the world it is loved, even before the child can do or become anything for their parents. This type of love excludes I love you "if." Most importantly, their child is loved even after they do things to disappoint. Let's be honest, babies do a lot of unlovely things the first few years; they cause sleep deprivation, mess diapers...some very messy, cry, spill, and throw up on shoulders just to name a few. It only gets worse from there. Let them grow into teenagers, and it often becomes even harder to love our children.

I've often asked parents who were dealing with rebellious teens, "where's the line?" When will you stop loving your child? What would your son or daughter have to do to stop being your son or daughter? Imagine your sixteen-year-old daughter came home with her new boyfriend "Puck". He is twenty-seven and belongs to a motorcycle gang. He has been in and out of prison for the last nine years. Your daughter announces she loves Puck and is leaving to go live on the road with him and the gang. Despite your protests, she leaves. Over the next few years everything you feared becomes reality. She becomes addicted to drugs, is sexually passed around from gang member to gang member, has multiple abortions, and begins to prostitute herself. At what point would you stop loving her, and when does she stop being your daughter?" The interesting thing, even though I've asked that question hundreds of times, every parent answers it the same, "NEVER." Not once has a parent said I would only love her until she did drugs, or slept with the third guy, or only if she came home and admitted she was wrong. It's the same unconditional love offered to us by God Himself. It's the whole point of Jesus' parable of the prodigal son in Luke 15:11-24.

> Jesus continued: "There was a man who had two sons. The younger one said to his father, 'Father, give me my share of the estate.' So he divided his property between them. "Not long after that, the younger son got together all he had, set off for a distant country and there squandered his wealth in wild living. After he had spent everything, there was a severe famine in that whole country, and he began to be in need. So he went and hired

himself out to a citizen of that country, who sent him to his fields to feed pigs. He longed to fill his stomach with the pods that the pigs were eating, but no one gave him anything. "When he came to his senses, he said, 'How many of my father's hired servants have food to spare, and here I am starving to death! I will set out and go back to my father and say to him: Father, I have sinned against heaven and against you. I am no longer worthy to be called your son; make me like one of your hired servants.' So he got up and went to his father. "But while he was still a long way off, his father saw him and was filled with compassion for him; he ran to his son, threw his arms around him and kissed him. "The son said to him, 'Father, I have sinned against heaven and against you. I am no longer worthy to be called your son.' "But the father said to his servants, 'Quick! Bring the best robe and put it on him. Put a ring on his finger and sandals on his feet. Bring the fattened calf and kill it. Let's have a feast and celebrate. For this son of mine was dead and is alive again; he was lost and is found.' So they began to celebrate."

Isn't it interesting that never in the story did the son stop being the son despite his poor performance? That's because his father did not love him with a "because" or "if" kind of love, but unconditionally. The parable of the Prodigal Son was intended to teach us about God's love for us. It's that same type of unconditional love that ought to exist between a husband and a wife.

Why is it that God offers us unconditional love, and parents offer their children unconditional love, but we offer our spouses "if" and "because" love? Where did we get this messed up notion that love for a spouse is meant to be conditional and performance based? No wonder when life happens and things change for the unexpected so many marriages end up on the rocks. We loved each other "if" and "because."

This is why it is so critical to find an indoor kind of love. Which means you'll have to date indoor dogs. People have determined that living primarily for themselves doesn't pay off. It leads to heartache and disappointment.

Right about now someone is thinking, "but my outdoor dog is so lovable! He or she has so many good qualities. I can fix my outdoor dog." You realize you've just admitted that your outdoor dog is a project, and I can predict where this endeavor lands you. It's not that an outdoor dog can never change; it's just that they seldom do, and it takes years. I wish I could introduce you to the hundreds of couples who have lined up outside my office over the years because one of them married their backyard dog confident they would change them. Now it's years later and their bet didn't pan out despite years of patience and effort. Exhausted and

> Marry someone who will work with you, not become your life's work.

79

ready to give up, they would all counsel you, "never risk your future on a backyard dog." If you're not careful you'll convince yourself your story is different than theirs. You'll date your backyard dog a couple more years, become tired of dating, and marry them. You'll continue to work on your backyard dog, which in many ways means you will be "the parent" in the relationship, and they'll resent you just like every teenager does. After a few years you'll have a couple kids... more projects! Eventually, you'll realize you're the only adult in the relationship. In essence you'll be a single parent waiting for both your spouse and your kids to grow up. How much more healthy to marry someone who's fully cooked? Your kids will be enough of a project, and you're going to want help raising them, not an extra kid. Another way of putting it, marry a minister not a ministry, marry someone who will work with you, not become your life's work.

This is why, if you find yourself in an "If" – "Because" relationship it's time to break with your backyard dog. If they are offering you conditional love, you don't want it! It will leave you heartbroken when they notice the prettier girl, the finances go south, or you don't perform up to expectations, and your backyard dog bolts for the gate.

Questions

1. Why do so many people get caught up in conditional love relationships?

2. Has someone ever loved you conditionally? How did it feel?

3. Is conditional love actually love? Why or why not?

4. What will you change based on what you've learned in this chapter?

ten

Indoor Love

This next chapter is the longest in the book. I thought it was critical we take a look at what indoor love looks like. I once heard that when the United States government is training agents to recognize counterfeit money, they don't spend much time exposing them to counterfeit bills; there are just too many variations to ever memorize. Instead, they train them to flawlessly recognize a real bill. That way when they encounter a counterfeit they immediately know it's not the real deal. This chapter is dedicated to the same idea. If I can help you recognize selfless love, maybe you can avoid settling for something less. I'd like to encourage you to bear down and work your way through it; you'll be glad you did, and the chapters that follow are worth the effort.

If you've ever attended a wedding, chances are somewhere in the ceremony 1 Corinthians 13 was read. It is often referred to as the love chapter. It contains an amazing description of love. The reason it is read at weddings is that we all intuitively know that the only way a long-term relationship like marriage has any hope for survival is if it's bathed in love. This is because no matter how wonderful the person we marry, they all come with a set of faults. If you decide to marry them, you will have simply chosen to deal with the particular faults your spouse brings to the relationship. No matter how trivial they seem in the beginning, there will come a day when those faults will stretch your patience and grate your nerves. Like a festering splinter, they will become increasingly irritating. That's where love kicks in, "Love covers a multitude of sins." Not because love is blind, but because love clearly sees the others faults and chooses to love in-spite of them.

This is why the backyard dog gets in trouble. The backyard dog selfishly loves himself or herself more than any other person. They "love" the person they are with because they get what they want from the relationship. It is the pinnacle of selfish behavior. True love is selfless love; the success of any long-term relationship will be in direct proportion to how well both you and your spouse have learned to become selfless lovers.

It's not that love is oblivious to the other's faults; that's infatuation not love. Love simply says I love you more than your faults. I hope you will grow beyond them, but even if you don't, I still love you. I am not in this relationship for what you can do for me (that's an I love you if/because kind of love) but because I love you more than I love me. That's why scripture prescribes:

> "Submit to one another out of reverence for Christ." Ephesians 5:21

Submitting is not about someone being the boss and the other the servant. It's about loving someone so much that you place his or her needs above your own. What is being "submitted" (or placed lower) is your desires. If you're doing that for someone else, you really do love him or her. It is exactly what Christ did on the cross. It's obvious when you read the story of Christ's prayer in the garden of Gethsemane the night before his death; he had no desire to die. He willingly submitted His desire to live to our need for a Savior. That's love... and great couples figure out how to submit to each other. Backyard dogs resist this.

This is why it is so interesting that we read 1 Corinthians 13 at so many weddings. Often as the attributes of selfless love are being listed, those in attendance at the wedding all know that the bride and groom don't possess anything close to what is being described. One or both are backyard dogs having spent their dating careers seeking their own selfish fulfillment above all else. Now they stand in front of a couple hundred close friends promising to try to behave like indoor dogs, and everyone in the crowd knows they are in serious trouble.

Let's take a closer look at 1 Corinthians 13 and consider what it would take to develop selflessness before your wedding day. It is equally critical to be able to identify selflessness in the person you date. Here's how the Bible describes selfless love:

> "Love is patient, love is kind. It does not envy,
> it does not boast, it is not proud. It does not
> dishonor others, it is not self-seeking, it is not
> easily angered, it keeps no record of wrongs.
> Love does not delight in evil but rejoices with
> the truth." 1 Corinthians 13:4-6

Patient: Love expresses itself by the giving of time. Selflessness says I hope we can work on the areas of your life that need growth, and it would be nice if we could fix this in short order, but I'm willing to invest whatever effort and take whatever time is necessary. Bottom line, your spouse will bring shortcomings to the marriage that they may never outgrow. Just ask my wife Lisa, after 33 years of marriage I'm still not as romantic as she would like. That's why it will require patience.

> Unsolicited advice is always viewed as criticism, and criticism is Kryptonite to a man.

It's amazing how many women go into marriage planning to fix their man. It's as if his mother has left him half-baked, and now it's her turn to finish the job. She immediately starts in on an improvement plan for him. What women don't realize is that men deeply resent this, and there is no more sure fire way to lose your man's heart. This is because in man culture, men NEVER offer unsolicited advice. Unsolicited advice is always viewed as criticism, and criticism is kryptonite to a man.

As an example let's use a hypothetical guy, we'll call him Jordan, who is outside working on his car. His friend who happens to be an accomplished mechanic will be standing there watching. Even though the mechanic friend has a pretty good idea what is wrong he will not offer advice. He will simply lend his presence and an occasional grunt or two. This is because in man culture to offer advice would be tantamount to calling him "dumb" and "incapable." To the heart of a man it sounds like, "hey, because you're so stupid and will never figure this out on you own let me tell you the answer." Men simply do not cross that line with each other, instead the friend waits till Jordan says, "I just can't figure this out, I've tried the sparkplugs, the carburetor looks fine, I'm getting a spark, I just don't know what to do next." That's the friend's cue that Jordan is open to input. Then and only then will he speak.

This is also why men refuse to ask for directions. In the heart of a man, figuring out how to get there gives him a deep sense of accomplishment. That sense of accomplishment is something he desires and is much, much more important to him than arriving on time.

Although the illustration may seem humorous to women, it speaks to the very heart of a man and underlines the need for her patience. She must be patient enough for him to either figure it out on his own or more importantly, until he asks for her advice. She knows the answer; she could fix him right now, but it is imperative she be selflessly patient and wait for him to be ready.

Selfishness wants what it wants when it wants it. This is why any girl whose boyfriend is pressuring her for sex should immediately recognize that; his impatience has NOTHING to do with love. Even if he says he just wants to show her how much he loves her, what he actually wants is to show her how much he loves himself, and how much he's willing to manipulate her to get his own selfish needs met. Having sex before marriage will immediately and deeply damage your relationship with God. That has nothing to do with what's best for you. What happened to submitting his needs to what is best for her? Love waits, because love is patient.

Kind: Kind means considerate. Selflessly considering the other's needs before your own. When my son was small, one night I woke to hear him coughing in the other room. To be honest at first I just laid there a while hoping he would stop. For me sleep is sacred; so, if there's anything I don't want interrupted, it's my sleep. Sure enough, a few moments later he coughed again. I listened; hoping to hear my wife, Lisa, had awakened and was headed to help him. You guessed it... she was sound asleep. Here's what I wrestled in that moment, I wanted my sleep but my son needed my help. So, I stumbled out of bed, braved the dark house, checked on him, and located the well-hidden cough syrup at the very bottom of the medicine drawer. Why is it that you find what you're looking for in the last place you look? I fumbled for a spoon, took it to his room, laid with him a while till he went back to sleep, then 45 minutes later shuffled back to my own bed. I went to my son not because I felt butterflies or goose bumps of love (at that moment I felt a lot of things, none of which were goose bumps) but because he needed something from me, and the kind thing to do was set aside my selfish desire for sleep in order to fulfill his need.

Guys, your wife will need you to be kind over and over again. As a matter of fact, it is how God wired her to receive love from you. Just look at what Peter has to say about the topic:

> "Husbands, in the same way be considerate as you live with your wives, and treat them with respect as the weaker (more delicate) partner and as heirs with you of the gracious gift of life, so that nothing will hinder your prayers." 1 Peter 3:7

Ever wonder why stories like Prince Charming and Snow White are so popular with girls. It's how they receive love. Every woman dreams of the man who will love her more than anything else, who will risk everything, and who will leverage his masculinity and strength for her benefit. That means being able to say to her, "I will not let anyone or anything harm you. I am here to protect you, and I would lay my life down for you. I will never use my strength against you." That's why it is such a huge betrayal when a man physically abuses a woman. The very one who promised to be her prince is now harming her. It doesn't mater if the harm is physical or verbal; it is still a heartbreaking betrayal of your promise. You need to be able to say, "I will not allow anything to hurt you, but if it ever does it will never be from my hand or my mouth, and I will avenge the wrong. I am your kind of prince."

> Every woman dreams of the man who will love her more than anything else, who will risk everything, and who will leverage his masculinity and strength for her benefit.

Ladies, if you're dating a guy who verbally abuses you, says hurtful words to win a fight, or God forbid has hit you, he is not your prince. Drop that backyard dog off at the Humane Society and let someone else adopt him.

Ladies, God may have given your male counterpart strength through which to express kindness to you, but he gave you beauty. There is something that is deeply attractive about the female form to guys, and guys are hugely visual. Kindness says I will never use my beauty to manipulate you or as a weapon to coerce you. This is why it is so wrong for you to overtly display your feminine assets in order to trap a man. We've all seen the young lady who dresses to leave nothing to the imagination. The reality is you will attract a man that way. Backyard dogs will come sniffing by the droves. Because backyard dogs know they can get what they want from a girl desperate enough to dress that way. The unkindness is you using your beauty and sexuality to lure a man to get what you want. This is actually deeply selfish and manipulative. A woman who coerces men with her sexuality will actually turn off a Godly man. He knows her clothes or lack thereof say something about her character. No wonder scripture says:

> "Like a gold ring in a pig's snout is a beautiful woman who shows no discretion." Proverbs 11:22

Lust is most men's inherent weakness. If he is going to fall in love with you, let it be for more than the outward package; don't use the wrapper as a weapon. Don't manipulate him with lust and wound his walk with Jesus so that he is out of fellowship with God in an effort to get what you want from him. I'm not suggesting you dress frumpy; every guy wants the person he is dating to be attractive, but there is a big difference between dressing attractively and dressing to attract. Gals, you know what I'm talking

> The problem with envy is that we never become a team because we are always competing against each other for the same position.

about. If you don't, flip open any fashion magazine, and you'll catch the difference.

Does not envy: In relationships envy most often shows up in the role of the front-runner. Who's the smartest, who's the more social, who makes the most money, or who's the most admired. Envy says it has to be me and can't rejoice in the success of the other person. The problem with envy is that we never become a team because we are always competing against each other for the same position.

My freshman year of Bible College I went out for our football team. Our school was small and had no scholarships so we were all walk-ons. I, of course, tried out for quarterback. Two other guys competed against me, and in the end it came down to just two of us. On the one hand you had Nate, who was a much better scrambler and had a stronger arm than me. I had a much better understanding of the offense and was a more accurate passer. In the end the coach gave the job to Nate. I couldn't believe it. What a poor decision. I actually began to question our coach's ability to lead the team. I spent the next few weeks rooting for Nate's failure. I reveled in every mistake from poorly executed plays to miss thrown passes. Surely a few more weeks of this and I'd have the job I so justly deserved. I was given the role of wide receiver. To help my situation, if Nate passed a ball a little out of my reach I never sped up or gave an extra effort; after all his failure would lead to my success. Despite all my best (or worst) efforts, the coach stuck with Nate. Though I could not figure out why for the life of me. Our team was struggling. It would be better with me at the helm.

Then it dawned on me, if we kept having bad practices, if I kept delivering a halfhearted effort to expose Nate's weaknesses, we were going to stay bad, and it was going to be a miserable season. So, I determined Nate was our quarterback and that his success was going to be the team's success. If we were going to lose, it would not be because I was still competing for Nate's position. I began to run every route with precision, dive for miss-thrown balls, and hold every block for all I was worth. When Nate made a mistake, I encouraged him. Sometimes on the sidelines I would walk him through a play we had messed up the series before.

Turned out, we were good; I mean really good. Our team went undefeated for the next two years. Some of my best memories are of playing on that team. But we only became a team when I stopped competing with my teammate.

If you're in a relationship it has to be okay for the person you're dating to be better than you are at something. You can't be competitive about who advances at work more quickly, who can tell the best story, or who has achieved more scholastically. And, sometimes even if you have done something bigger or better, shut up about it, let them have their time in the sun. Give them their own moment of glory even if it's smaller than yours. If you truly love them selflessly you won't envy their success. If you are truly a team, their success is your success. Love doesn't envy.

Does not boast: Boasting is all about stealing the spotlight. Boasting says look at me, someone really important is sitting over here, and you are not paying enough attention to me. The problem with fighting for all the attention means you have to steal it from your mate. It's as if you're saying, "Boy, are you lucky to be with me!" Your achievements are so minimal in comparison you should probably feel inferior in my presence. Selfless love lifts up the person they are with. It looks for the opportunity to point out their virtues and strengths instead of their own. Often this is terrifying for us because we believe they will get big headed and they will wonder what they are doing with us. Ironically, just the opposite is true; you and I are deeply attracted to people who see value in us. It is an amazing expression of love; this is why parents often intuitively ask their child's suitor, what do you like about my son/daughter. What parents understand is this, the more insightful the answer, the more likely there is a substantial love behind it. Selfless love sees the best about the other person and not themselves.

Ladies, this is especially important for you to master, because one of the core needs of a man is admiration. This is why little boys play super hero, army, and video games. Their deepest desire is to be the hero. He's really hoping to be your hero. There is nothing more powerful you can do than to brag on him in front of your friends. It lets him know he's on the right track, and you might just be the one who lets him be a hero. This also reflects back on the idea of love being patient and women being careful not to offer unsolicited advice or criticism to a male, especially publicly. There is no more sure fire way to turn his heart away than to criticize him. Every man wants to be admired.

When my son Josh was nine we were running some errands together. As we were driving along quietly he blurted out, "I hate living in Chandler, Arizona." "Why," I asked, "We have a great home here, you have a ton of friends, and you're doing well in school. Why don't you like living here?" His response,

> Sometimes love is silent.

"It's not like anything is ever going to happen here. We will never get attacked by terrorist or anything." As a male, I immediately knew what my young son was trying to express. He might never have the opportunity to be a hero!

Every man hopes for that opportunity. Most of us realize we'll probably never save millions of people, but when we choose a wife we hope to be her hero. That's why her criticism is especially wounding. It says, "your failing." Selfless love lifts up the person. Sometimes lifting up is consciously choosing not to point out a fault. Sometimes... love is silent.

Is not proud: Some of us can't remember the last time we walked into a room and didn't immediately think we were the smartest most capable person in the room. The surprising thing is no one else seemed to notice. When is the last time you said, "you know what, you're right, and I am wrong." Some of us can't work for anyone else, because no one is capable of properly supervising an individual of our caliber. If this describes you then bottom line is you're prideful, and this should terrify you. Prideful people are horrible at relationships. Consider what the wisest man in the world said about pride:

> "Where there is strife, there is pride,"
> Proverbs 13:10a

Isn't it interesting that Solomon, a guy who had every right to be proud, said that prideful people cause strife relationally? Some of us grew up in homes with a father who could not admit he was wrong to save his life. He was right about everything, just ask him, and doubly so when he was wrong. Others grew up with moms who had to be seen as super mom at everything from cleaning the house to snacks for the soccer team, and that prideful quest to be perfect drove a wedge in the entire family as they strove to be perfect so she would appear perfect to others.

If you've ever lived with a prideful person you know it is horribly destructive. If you are prideful, your pride will hinder every relationship in your life. The last thing you want to do is date a proud person because their behavior will always lead both of you to heartache.

"Pride goes before destruction, a haughty spirit before a fall." Proverbs 16:18

Note this verse doesn't say sometimes or often. Proud people inevitably set a course for their lives, and for anyone around them that will be painful.

Love is not rude: This is a really important attribute of love that is often misunderstood. Bible translators have struggled to put the original Greek word into English. In Greek it is the word ασχημονει. The King James Version translates it "unseemly" and the NIV "rude." But ασχημονει more appropriately should be translated "dishonoring." The thought of Bible translators was, if you dishonor someone then you're being rude. But that's not what the apostle Paul meant when he wrote 1 Corinthians. He wasn't saying "I won't be rude to you," but instead he meant, "I won't be dishonoring with you." In other words love never asks the other to do or participate in something that would bring dishonor or shame to their life. Love says, "I will not pressure you to do something that might bring you future regret."

Which means, ladies, if he pressures you, if he says, "if you love me, you'll let me." That pressure has absolutely NOTHING to do with love. If he loves you, he will not dishonor you and your Heavenly Father by pressuring you to do something that would be sinful. Instead, his request is the howling of a backyard dog and has everything to do with being selfish.

Guys, I don't care if she offers herself to you. If you love her, you will say, "NO, NO, NO. I'm not going to do anything with you physically while we're dating that might potentially end up being a part of your future regret, and I love you too much to take you until we're married because that would be selfish of me."

A friend told me this story. "I remember when I was dating my wife. Things were going great, and we were moving forward in the relationship. I had no doubts she was the one. There was this one-day, we were together having a tickling fight. In the middle of all the tickling, Things began to happen...you know what I'm saying! In that moment I had to make a decision because I knew exactly where things were headed. I also knew she cared about me enough that I could have coerced her. So, all of the sudden I stopped tickling her. She asked, "What's wrong?" To which I replied, "Nothing." She said, "NO! What's wrong with you?" I answered, "Nothing." "No" she demanded, "why aren't we tickling some more." So I told her… It was a really awkward conversation; I had to tell her that things were happening for me physically. I was beginning to want to do things we shouldn't be doing. It's interesting because we're married now, and my wife tells that story over and over and over to our friends. She says that was when she knew for certain she had met a man of honor and that I really loved her." Love does not dishonor or create future regret. Jim got it right!

Is not self-seeking: This means no private agendas. It's not a competition! Self-seeking people have an innate need to win. It's their idea, their plan, and their thought that has to prevail. Prevail above all others, not because it's best, but because it's theirs. If you're a self-seeking individual then your idea of the perfect spouse is finding someone with no opinions so you can run the show.

You might ask, "How can it work, if neither person is at least a little self seeking? How do you ever make a decision? If both people are constantly deferring to the other how do you even choose a restaurant let alone a car, or a vacation?" Being selfless doesn't mean that you become a wet noodle and just do whatever the other person wants; it simply means you don't insist on what you want. You stop running decisions through the filter of what's best for you or what you would decide if

> Being selfless does not mean that you become a wet noodle and just do whatever the other person wants; it simply means you don't insist on what you want.

you were still single and begin to run them through the filter of what's best for us.

Is not easily angered: This is different than patience. Patience was about giving time for growth. Anger is about your personal maturity. It requires the ability to agree to disagree without blowing your top. Selfless love means you will not pull out verbal weapons in order to win a fight. You are never to say a hurtful thing in order to gain a tactical advantage during an argument. Most of us know exactly what to say to the person we're dating, especially if we've dated them for a while, to inflict the maximum harm. When you do that you are no longer arguing to fix, you are fighting to win, which means the person you're dating has to be the loser, and that simply has nothing to do with love. One of the most critical tests for the person you are dating to pass is how they treat you when they disagree with you. Do they treat you with respect and honor in the midst of the discussion all the while working toward a solution and not a victory? Or, do they wound and manipulate to get their own way?

At our church, I hired an incredibly high-powered woman for one of our executive roles. I hired her because she was an overachiever. If I gave her an assignment, she was going to get it done! Her husband is a really strong, opinionated guy. He has an idea about everything, and he's pretty sure his idea is right. Chances are if you had helped with their pre-marital counseling, you might have advised them not to get married. How do two super strong individuals co-exist in the same relationship? Who wins and how bloody is the loser? The answer is neither and not at all. They have learned how to be selfless.

One day she described for me the typical disagreement in their home. She said, "You know, every once in a while my husband and I end up going back and forth with some intensity. But, something I've learned is that if I'm willing to be the one who extends the olive branch and will go along with his idea, something remarkable happens. Almost every time, he comes back later and says to me, 'You know if it's that important to you, I think we ought to do it your way'." Her gesture of selflessness is met with a softening of his heart.

What just happened? The answer is that two very strong people have learned to contain their anger by putting the other first. Anger is all about me not getting my way, or you not behaving how I suggested. In contrast, she has learned to be selfless enough to concede before their words and actions cause harm. She has decided that no matter how right she feels it simply is not worth the potential damage that insisting on winning the argument might cause. Rather than getting angry because her way is not being heeded, she blesses her husband with concession, which leaves no room for anger on her part. He in turn has learned to selflessly put her desires above his own. He loves her more than he loves being right. Rather than angrily insisting on his own way he has discovered it actually brings him joy to please her. Are you and your partner willing to practice what it takes to become indoor dogs?

Keeps no records of wrongs: A record of wrongs is most apparent when the past keeps being brought up and rehashed over and over again. Even though it has been talked through, somehow the rotting corpses of past wrongs keep emerging from their grave. This will be the death of any relationship. If you keep scoreboards of the offenses done to you, eventually the person you are dating will reach your limit. Even if your limit is really big, eventually they will get there. And, when they do, the relationship will turn toxic. Everything they do from then on will disgust you. The way he slurps, the flick, flick, flick of her fingernails, his "silent" burp.

I've counseled countless couples that by the time they came to me, the scoreboard was full. At that point there is nothing I can say. There is nothing their husband or wife can do. Their limit has been exceeded, and there's no room for grace left on the board. In relationships where someone keeps a running tally of wrongs, ultimately their spouse ends up exceeding the limit, and full scoreboards remove all potential for the relationship to move forward.

The answer is no running tally of wrongs. If the person you are dating has done something that bothers you or hurts your heart, deal with it. Don't just tell them about it, or argue till you're tired. Commit to working toward a solution. You're not finished until you fix it... fix it and forgive it. The only good scoreboard is at a football game. We are commanded to keep our scoreboards as clean as God's:

> "Be kind and compassionate to one another,
> forgiving each other, just as in Christ God
> forgave you." Ephesians 4:32

That's why in healthy relationships you're not finished with a topic until you conclude with forgiveness.

Does not delight in evil, but rejoices in the truth: This is all about deception. Love does not deceive the one it loves. This can be hard because dating is all about putting your best foot forward. The problem is that if the person you're dating never sees the real you, when they begin to have genuine feelings you will live in the constant fear that they actually love the person you've pretended to be.

I dated a girl for over a year and was actually thinking about proposing. The interesting thing is about that time some of our mutual friends began to say to me, Linn we are really surprised you are getting so serious about Kim (not her real name). She seems so different from who we picture you with. They then pointed out things I had never seen in her. None of which were necessarily bad things but things I would not have chosen in my wife. So, I began to watch more closely, and sure enough, my friends were right. Kim had taken all the things about herself that she sensed I didn't like and had neatly tucked them away. She was being someone completely different than the real Kim. She was acting the way she sensed I wanted her to be. That discovery led to a lot of talking and honesty; we eventually broke up. I thank God every day for friends who cared

> The really powerful thing is that if you choose to pay the price to be an indoor dog yourself, you will suddenly be able to spot other indoor dogs.

enough to say something, and that I eventually married someone who was exactly right for me. Be who you really are with the people you date so that when they fall in love, they'll be in love with you. Love does not trick someone into loving them.

Selfless love is all about the journey of becoming an indoor dog. The really powerful thing is that if you choose to pay the price to be an indoor dog yourself, you will suddenly be able to spot other indoor dogs. Selfless love is lots of work, and once you put in the work, you will readily see those same traits in others who have learned the lessons it takes to be an indoor dog.

Questions

1. In your last relationship that went bad, which attributes of selfless love were missing in you and in them?

2. What do you think about during a wedding ceremony?

3. How do you hope your future spouse deals with your faults, failures, and imperfections?

4. Which of the attributes of selfless love is the hardest for you to practice in a relationship?

   A. Patient
   B. Kindness
   C. Does not envy
   D. Does not boast
   E. Is not proud
   F. Love is not rude, is not dishonoring with you
   G. Is not self-seeking
   H. Is not easily angered
   I. Keeps no records of wrongs
   J. Doesn't delight in evil but rejoices in truth

11. What is something you could do today that would be a step in the right direction to develop this attribute?

12. What will you begin to do differently because of this chapter?

Indoor Dogs Who Date Outdoor Dogs

eleven

Leaving Jesus Out

If you're an indoor dog, then you are a Christ follower. You've decided that He is important and you've committed to following Him with each decision you make in life. The problem comes when an indoor dog dates an outdoor dog. Outdoor dogs come in two breeds, they can be either non-Christians or they can be Christians who have chosen to live an outdoor lifestyle. Non-Christians aren't necessarily bad people; they are simply pre-Jesus. They haven't figured out what they believe about Jesus and where He fits into their life. The dilemma is, they may never figure it out! The second breed, Christians who choose to live a backyard lifestyle are just as dangerous. No one is going to tell them how to live their life. They are going to poop where they want to poop, dig where they want to dig, and chew what they want to chew. He/she may be a Christian, but Jesus clearly isn't their Lord.

Indoor dogs make a terrible mistake when they date outdoor dogs. Surprisingly, it's the outdoor dog that is in the most trouble for dating the indoor dog; this is because he or she is being duped. They think they are getting someone who is a kindred spirit. Someone committed to living the rest of their lives with the same recklessness and rebellion they possess. The Bible actually explains why this won't work long term:

"Can two walk together except they be agreed?" Amos 3:3

The passage is meant to be rhetorical; the obvious answer is NO. Simply put, if you're going on a walk with someone, and one of you wants to head North to the lake and the other wants to head South to the general store, you can't walk together unless someone changes their plans. This is even truer when it comes to Christ. If one person in the relationship is committed to living for Jesus, and the other one doesn't even know Jesus there is no way possible for you to walk together. Someone is going to have to change his or her mind or at the very least, their lifestyle. Since the non-Christian doesn't even know Christ there is no way possible for them to choose to bring Christ into the dating relationship. If these two are going to date, the Christian is the one who will have to change. The Christian will need to decide to leave Christ out during the courtship. Yah, yah...I know what you are going to say, you're missionary dating! At just the right time, you're going to inject Jesus into your conversations and hopefully... eventually, with enough pressure from you, your backyard dog will come around. OK, but how much Jesus will they tolerate... 1%, 2%? What about the other 98% of your dating? You'll have to behave like God isn't important; you'll have to leave God out, because they don't know God. 98% of your

> Since the non-Christian doesn't even know Christ there is no way possible for them to choose to bring Christ into the dating relationship.

relationship will be Godless; what you share won't have God in it. It won't be anything like a relationship with a legitimate Christ follower, will it? So, in the end, …it will be a 2% Christ centered relationship. Kind of feels like you're leaving God out doesn't it?

Here's why that's super unfair to the non-Christian. While you were dating, while you were trying to "hook" them, you had to move in the direction of behaving like a backyard dog/backslidden Christian. Sold out Christians don't put God on the back burner for a date; all the while hoping to covertly change them into an indoor dog.

> She thought she was marrying Kanye West and now you've turned out to be Billy Graham.

The problem is we marry the people we date. You'll eventually find yourself falling in love with your backyard dog. Ultimately, you get married and have kids. You'll run out of time for pretending; kids are in the mix! Kids change everything, and you will want them raised with values. You will want to know they have made a decision for Christ and are headed to heaven. You will want them to date better than you. Time for that backyard dog to be housebroken! So, you'll apply the pressure. You'll head back to church, join a couple's Bible study and tell your backyard dog they need to fall in line and attend with you.

If I'm a backyard dog, I'm crying "foul." "This isn't what I signed up for. I figured we would party into our 70's, and instead I wake up one day to Mother Teresa. She thought she was marrying Kanye West, and now you've turned out to be Billy Graham. In truth you're the one who has been deceptive; you sold them a Christian version of Florida swampland. You were willing to take a spiritual detour, but your intent was always to eventually get back on the right track, which means as far as your backyard dog is concerned, your dating life was a lie. What they believed they were getting when they hooked up with you ended up being a scam. You have defrauded them and sold them a bill of goods that you didn't deliver.

If you're a non-Christian reading this book, and you're dating a Christian, get out of Dodge while the getting is good. Let me explain why. The Christian you're dating may have legitimately decided to walk away from Christ in order to pursue a relationship with you. The problem is, in all likelihood your Christian is going to change back. You see, when they became a Christian, the Holy Spirit (God in Spirit) came to live in their heart. When He did this, something about them was forever changed. Changed so completely that the Bible describes that moment as "born again." This means that he or she is forever a child of God and like any good parent when a child goes wayward, God is going to pursue, and believe me, God is relentless. Simply put, that Christian you are dating will most likely repent. They will suddenly get deadly serious about God, and then they are going to want to change you. The partying will be over. They'll start quoting Bible verses to you. You'll be stuck. So run...run while you can!

Questions

1. What are some ways Christians pretend like Jesus doesn't matter in relationships?

2. Why is it dangerous for both the Christian and non-Christian to date?

3. Is it ever right for a Christian to date someone who doesn't know Jesus?

4. What is your take away from this chapter?

twelve

The Yoke Principle

Again, the problem with dating a backyard dog is that you are likely to marry your backyard dog. Backyard dogs will grow on you, and eventually you'll settle. Any time you enter into a relationship with a backyard dog, whether it's a significant friendship or a marriage, you are "yoking" yourself to that backyard dog. The term yoked is a farming term. Before tractors, the most valuable asset any farmer could have was a matched team of oxen to pull his plow. The ideal was two animals of equal strength and equal stamina. Even with equality there were huge amounts of training required to teach the oxen to pull at the same pace with equal effort. When the training was completed, it was worth all the effort because a matched set could pull a plow all day long in a straight line with minimal effort on the farmer's part. Relationships are yoking!

I want to be clear here. I'm not suggesting that Christians shouldn't be friends with those who don't know Christ or are backslidden. As a Christian, chances are your friendship is someone's best hope to ever connect to Christ. It's when the Christian becomes dependent on the non-Christian that a relationship moves out of bounds. A friendship moves into dependence when you allow the input of someone who doesn't know Jesus to affect your decisions. If you are wondering if you've become yoked, ask this simple question, "If they were removed from your life would you feel weaker for their absence?" In that moment you're yoked. It's impossible to have a healthy dating relationship, and not be yoked.

> "Do not be yoked together with unbelievers. For what do righteousness and wickedness have in common? Or what fellowship do righteousness and wickedness have in common? Or what fellowship can light have with darkness? What harmony is there between Christ and Belial? What does a believer have in common with an unbeliever? What agreement is there between the temple of God and Idols? For we are the temple of the living God. As God has said, "I will live in them and walk among them, and I will be their God, and they will be me people. Therefore come out from among them, and be separate, says the Lord." 2 Corinthians 6:14-17a

If you entertain a relationship with a non-Christian or a backslidden believer, you will be moving in opposing directions. It will be an exhausting undertaking. No farmer would have settled for an unmatched set. One of the oxen would perpetually need to be spurred on to pull harder. The other oxen would require the farmer to apply constant drag to prevent it from getting ahead. All the while the farmer is attempting to steer the plow straight down the furrows. No wonder a matched set was so desirable. To try and help us understand the dilemma of dating backyard dogs, God uses the analogy of being "yoked" to them. It's because the problems of dating unsaved or backslidden people is identical to the unmatched team of oxen. Pair a Christian who is trying to follow God with someone who's not, and it will be grueling for both. One will try to make decisions for the pair based on trusting God; the other will be trusting in their own human capacity or worldly wisdom. The Christian will tend to forgive a wrong suffered, and the non-Christian will be more interested in seeking revenge. One may want to tithe, but one will be more interested in purchasing new toys. One will think Sundays are for attending church and honoring God, while the other will think Sundays are their last chance to rest before a busy workweek begins, and on and on the list goes. No wonder churches are full of Christians who in a season of naivety bound their life to someone who did not feel about God like they did. Now life is disappointing as they try to "pull" along their spouse. Although 2 Corinthians makes it clear a Christian is to never date or marry a non-believer or a backslidden Christian. I believe the principle is just as salient for dating Christians who are significantly behind in Christian maturity. If a strong believer dates a weak or baby Christian it will be almost impossible to make collaborative life decisions. If God is calling a man to the mission field, and his wife is a baby Christian, all the sacrifices and discomfort involved will most likely be more than she can accept even though she sincerely loves God in her baby level maturity.

> Why in the world would any woman choose a Chihuahua to lead her home?

Rather than being a help to him on the field, he'll either need to differ and concede to her trepidation and ignore God's call or drag her along despite her hesitations.

This dilemma becomes even more pronounced when a woman marries a man who is significantly less mature in the Lord. Picture two dogs; one is a Great Dane and the other a Chihuahua. Now yoke those two dogs together. From the moment they are strapped together that paring will be disastrous, and I feel sorry for the Chihuahua. This is exactly what happens when a mature Christian woman yokes herself to a baby Christian man. That poor guy is in for a dragging. The irony is, as bad as it is for him, it has to be equally exhausting for her. She has made him the head of her home. Consequently she must now submit to his leadership as he makes baby mistake upon baby mistake. She can see the right answers that he can't. When she expresses her concern, he thinks she is being controlling and criticizing. If she muscles her way into the lead, she's disobeying God. Why in the world would any woman choose a Chihuahua to lead her home?

Questions

1. Describe the yoking principle in your own words.

2. Why is it important for a farmer to pick an equal pair for yoking?

3. Would you be the Great Dane or the Chihuahua in a relationship as of today? Why?

4. What are some values a Christian and a non-Christian are likely to disagree about?

5. Why is it important to find a partner with a similar spiritual maturity?

thirteen

Shaky Foundations

Jesus taught the lesson of the wise builders, He said:

"Therefore everyone who hears these words of
mine and puts them into practice is like a wise
man who built his house on the rock. The rain
came down, the streams rose, and the winds
blew and beat against that house; yet it did not
fall, because it had it's foundation on the rock.
But everyone who hears these words of mine
and does not put them into practice is like a
foolish man who built his house on the sand.
The rain came down, and the streams rose, and
the winds blew and beat against that house,
and it fell with a crash." Matthew 7:24-27

The obvious teaching of this passage is that people who
build their lives on a foundation other than Jesus make a
huge mistake. But, don't miss the fact that Jesus affirms that
foundations are critical for our success. This is especially true
of the foundations we choose in dating relationships. Like
the three little pigs chose three different materials for their
homes, you and I have three different "materials" to build
as the foundation for our relationships: sex, friendship, God.

You've probably already guessed God would want you to
build every relationship, especially a dating relationship that

might result in marriage, on Him. In an indoor dog relationship the passionate unwavering devotion two Christians possess becomes the first thing that attracts them to each other. This common commitment to God establishes the basis for how they behave with each other, where they go or don't go physically, the filter through which they make joint decisions, and the very basis from which they determine if they are a good long term match for each other. If you're dating someone, how much do you pray together? Do you discuss the future in terms of what you believe God is planning for your lives, and do those God given plans make sense for you together? Does he intend to be a missionary and she feels led to stay near her parents to help out? When you make a decision in your relationship, is God at the center of those plans? Putting God first should form the very foundation of a strong Christian relationship. Picture a pyramid with the lower third representing the couple's commitment to God as the foundation on which the rest of the relationship will be built upon.

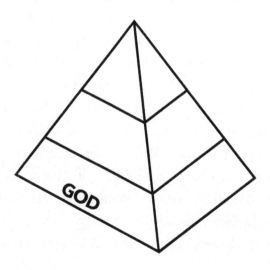

The second layer of a good relationship is friendship. Do we enjoy similar things? Do our differences actually compliment each other to create the synergy of a team or do our differences create friction and antagonism? We've all seen people who were highly physically attracted to each other but who fought like cats and dogs often over the most trivial things. In contrast, people who are together and super compatible socially often describe their relationship as "she's my best friend." "I just loved being with him...one day I realized it wasn't just being with him I loved... I loved him.

My son recently got married to an amazing gal named Amy. They both had a love of music, witty personalities, and a love for Jesus. One of the greatest joys Lisa and I share is watching them interact. They are very playful with each other. They effortlessly treat each other with kindness. Both of them are highly intelligent, and often they tease using sarcasm, but there is always a loving smile attached. My guess is that that much playfulness between a man and a woman translates into other parts of their marriage, if you know what I mean. Don't sell short the benefits of actually liking the person you're going to spend the rest of your life with. If you're considering marrying someone you're highly attracted to but you spend a lot of time fighting, are you actually friends? Would you choose this person for your inner circle if you weren't dating them? If you're not in "like" with them are you really in love with them, or just in lust with them? Having a strong friendship that says, "I like and enjoy you as a person", "I would be your friend, even if we weren't dating," is a big deal!

The tip of the iceberg, so to speak, is a strong sexual attraction for the person you're dating. I haven't left this till last because it isn't important, it really is! Believe me, I am HIGHLY attracted to my wife, Lisa. You don't ever want to marry someone who doesn't elicit a strong physical response for you. When you are together butterflies should fly and tingles should ting. Sex and all that goes with it is one of God's most incredible gifts to a man and a woman. At it's best; the sexual interaction between a man and woman really is lovemaking. I hope when you find the right person you are so attracted to them that you can hardly keep your hands off each other. With that said; remaining physically pure during your dating will be a monumental test of your devotion to Christ. That kind of attraction will go a long way to easing the rough spots of your first years of marriage. The reason it is last is because it doesn't matter how physically attracted you are to someone if they haven't met the first two foundations. A man can look at a pornographic image of a woman and be highly attracted to her. That in no way makes her the right one for him. A woman can see an amazingly attractive man and feel all sorts of butterflies, and yet he might be the biggest jerk in the room. Believe me, I've seen plenty of amazing women date really sketchy men because of their looks and confidence. So, simply put, keep your hormones on a leash until you know the person who excites you loves God, and you actually like them as a person, then attract away. For an example of a healthy relationship note the illustration below:

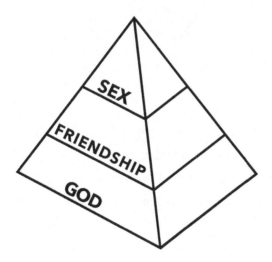

Unfortunately, backyard dogs want to turn the pyramid upside down. They want sex to be the basis for the relationship. They mistakenly believe that their inverted pyramid based on a strong physical connection is substantial enough to face the storms of life. Picture a pyramid turned upside down and balanced on its tip. The pyramids in Egypt, which have withstood eons of time, wouldn't have lasted a week turned upside down. Relationships with sex as its key component are too unstable to last.

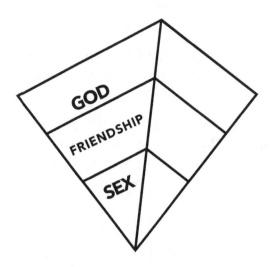

Jason was a good-looking guy and by the end of his sophomore year had dated nearly every cheerleader at his Bible College. Then came a beautiful transfer student named Jill. Jason and Jill were immediately an item. It was very clear from the beginning that there was tons of sexual attraction. There were a lot of evenings spent on the back porch of Jason's apartment away from the prying eyes of his roommates. A few short months later Jason announced that they were getting married. Friends thought it was a little too fast, so much of their relationship seemed to center on the physical, but they met at Bible College, and they were both Christians, what could go wrong?

Five years and a daughter later, Jill cheated on Jason. He and Jill had been living in Colorado and attending church where Jill's father was the pastor. She had been spending a lot of time with a guy who was an old high school friend. Whenever anyone would ask Jason how he felt about his wife spending so much time with another man, he would assure them that he trusted her implicitly. Then one day her father, the pastor, visited their home in the middle of the day while Jason was at work. He noticed the other man's car parked outside. He entered the home to find Jill and the other guy in bed together. Imagine being discovered by your own dad, the pastor!

Jason and Jill agreed to stay together and work on the marriage. They would move out of state and get a fresh start. Several weeks later they moved in together with an old buddy from Bible College. Jason and Ryan mowed lawns together to pay the bills, Jill stayed home to watch her and Jason's daughter. You have never seen a man more attentive or caring to his wife than Jason was. He was going to do whatever was necessary to put his marriage back together. He took Jill on regular dates, constantly showed affection and appreciation. He was an amazing dad to their daughter. He was the poster child for "Husband of the Year."

After a while, Jill began leaving during the day. She would get dressed up and find a babysitter so she could go "shopping." Eventually she confessed that she had been having a second affair with a new man. When Jason asked why, she simply replied, "Because it was wrong." She had spent her life being the perfect pastor's daughter and now she wanted to experience the dark side. She loved the rush that came with being "bad." It's why she was physical with Jason before the wedding, why she cheated in Colorado, why she cheated after they moved. Bottom line, sex is never enough of a foundation for a relationship.

WHY A SEX-FIRST RELATIONSHIP IS DOOMED

A sex first relationship is doomed from the start for several reasons. First, sex is the end zone celebration of a relationship. Sex is what you do when your relationship is scoring touchdowns. That's why it can never be the basis for a great relationship; sex is the result of... not the basis for... a great relationship. If the other parts of your relationship are struggling, sex makes no sense. It's like cheering when you're losing the game. If the kids are out of control, if finances are abysmal and one spouse is overspending, or if you're arguing about vacation plans, believe me, sex is the last thing on your wife's mind. When the sex cools off in a sex first relationship, the very reason you are together is now non-existent. I can't tell you how many men get into a marriage because the sex is great. Then real life comes a knocking, along with a couple of kids and an intrusive mother-in-law. His wife doesn't want to have sex because there is nothing to celebrate, and he's left wondering, "why did I even get married, and where has all the sex gone?" That husband will become ever increasingly frustrated. Chances are the thing that brought them together, sex, will now be the number one thing that drives a wedge in the relationship. It's the plight of an upside down pyramid. If they were putting God first, if they were great friends facing

> Sex is the end zone celebration of a relationship.

the harder parts of life as a team, there would still be wins to celebrate, and the sex would be running smoothly.

The second reason sex is a lousy foundation is because we all get old. I know this is hard for you to believe, but he won't look like he does now twenty years from now. Her body right now is bangin', but chances are it will look different over time. Gravity has a way of winning, and things begin to change position. How many times have you looked at your grandparents and wondered, "how could they possibly have ever been sexually attracted to each other?" The other day, Lisa was showing me a picture of one of her high school classmates.

> Things sag that used to be firm, hair grows where hair has no business growing, and hair stops growing where it needed to stay.

My comment, "Boy, she has not aged well." "She looks more our parents age than ours." I wonder how many of my classmates have said the same about me. The truth is, time and age catch up with all of us, and if the basis of your relationship is primarily physical, there will be a day when the person you married does not look like the person in the wedding pictures. Things get bigger that shouldn't. Things sag that used to be firm, hair grows where hair has no business growing, and hair stops growing where it needs to stay. And, just like that our bodies change. If your relationship is based on your mate's physical appearance, your relationship will change too.

Finally, you don't want to base your relationship on the physical because there will always be someone out there younger and more attractive. You may be the most attractive person in the youth group, or at your school, or in your town, but the day is coming when someone more attractive will walk into the room. Just ask the Queen in Snow White. You may have been happy to snag him based on your good looks, and kept him there by

> You've reinforced his lust and taught him women can be bedded outside of marriage, and now you want him to behave like an indoor dog?

having sex with him, but all you've really done is taught him that beautiful women are available to him outside of marriage. Now, what do you do when "she" walks into the room, and he stares? You see the stare; it's how he used to look at you. How much jealousy wells up inside? How insecure do you feel in that moment? And…you should. Your entire relationship is based on sex, now a sportier model just became available. You've reinforced his lust and taught him that women can be bedded outside of marriage, and now you want him to behave like an indoor dog?

Good luck with that.

The relationship pyramid also demonstrates why it is a bad idea to date a non-Christian. Remember when a Christian dates a non-Christian, God has to be left out, or at the very least be minimized. At that point, there is no way God is the foundation for the relationship. The best they can hope for is second best by making friendship the basis of their marriage. They really do love spending time together; they are so close they can complete each other's sentences.

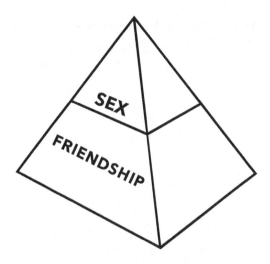

The problem is, humans change over time. We grow emotionally, and our interests transition from playing in the back yard to hanging out at the mall; skateboarding becomes video gaming. Remember third grade? If you are a girl, chances are you went home every day, your best friend came over, and you spent countless hours playing dolls. Years went by, and you and your friend were like sisters. Then the dreaded day, one of you discovered boys and suddenly dolls seemed juvenile. My bet is that one of you made the evolution before the other. Chances are, your friendship didn't survive the transition. One of you wanted to hang out where there were boys, and the other wanted to keep the relationship as it was - playing dolls. Both of you thought the other was stupid. The reality is almost none of us have the same friends we had in elementary school; friendships no matter how strong simply lose steam because what we once held in common changed.

Your relationship with an unsaved person today may seem even stronger than your friendship in elementary school, but things transition. Today you both love sci-fi movies, alternative music, and sunsets. The problem is you probably won't like all those things in the future. Lisa and I used to snow ski together; we haven't been in years. We used to go on shopping adventures looking for antiques to decorate our house, and today there are no antiques in our home. I don't tell you this to depress you; it is just a reality of life that we evolve and very seldom at the same rate as our spouse. If all you have to base your relationship on is your similarities socially, there is a high probability you will "fall out of love."

> You'll often hear, "we simply fell out of love." Not really, they simply built their love on something that changed.

Ever wonder why so many couples divorce after twenty plus years of marriage when the kids head off to college? Most often it's not because some catastrophic event occurred within the marriage. More likely, the event that spells death is the kids moving out. This is because it was a socially based marriage. Over the years, the things that originally drew them together changed. They used to like going to the theatre, and now he can't stand it. But they always had the kids in common. Getting them raised was a shared cause. Now they're gone, and seemingly the reason for being together moved out too. You'll often hear, "we simply fell out of love." Not really, they simply based their love on something that changed. That's why building your relationship on God is so wise:

> "Jesus Christ is the same yesterday and today and forever." Hebrews 13:8

My encouragement, be the wise man/woman, do exactly what Jesus encouraged you to do, build your relationship on Him.

Questions

1. What are the three foundations for a relationship?

2. What happens if you change the order of the pyramid?

3. Why is being someone's friend an important part of a dating relationship?

4. How does this chapter affect whom you date and/or how you act in relationships?

fourteen

The Dog Bed

When it comes to sex, culture is encouraging you to become a backyard dog. We are inundated every day with sexual images. Lyrics of songs tell us everyone else is doing it. Plots to movies champion that sex is how we become a real man or woman; that having sex is just two bodies rubbing together for mutual gratification. You and I have been told we are simply highly evolved animals that can have sex with no attachments to get in the way. That sex is purely a physical experience meant for physical gratification.

Have you ever been on a walk in your neighborhood, turned a corner, and stumbled across two dogs engaged in sex? It's kind of an awkward moment. Something inside says you need to look away. That response of embarrassment is a purely human reaction and in direct contrast to what culture teaches about sex. Culture says you are like those dogs. Dogs don't get embarrassed, and they are not embarrassed that you walked up on them. Think about it, dogs don't turn red and they can have sex with no real connection. They move from partner to partner indiscriminately, after all it's "just sex." To a dog there is no reason to be modest or wait till marriage because there is nothing intimate about the act. The reason you feel uncomfortable at the sight of two dogs is because you are not a dog! That blush on your cheeks is the very image of

God on your soul, and because you are a human created in the image of God, sex can never just be sex.

If you're not careful you'll accept the world's invitation to frolic in the backyard; you'll buy in to the lies that sex is purely a physical thing to be explored and enjoyed between two consenting adults. When the sex is over or the relationship runs its course you can walk away and be unchanged. In reality you'll discover that when you've treated sex like a dog does, something in your personhood has been deeply violated by the experience.

> That blush on your cheeks is the very image of God on your soul, and because you are a human created in the image of God, sex is never just sex.

For a human, the dog bed is very expensive. God explains why in 1 Corinthians 6:13b, 15-19. Pay special attention to verse 18:

> "...the body is not meant for sexual immorality, but for the Lord, and the Lord for the body. Do you not know that your bodies are members of Christ himself? Shall I take the members of Christ and unite them to a prostitute? Never! Do you not know that he who unites himself with a prostitute is one with her in body? For it is said, "The two will become one flesh." But he who unites himself to the Lord is one with him in spirit. Flee sexual immorality. All other sins a man

commits are outside the body but he who sin sexually sins against his own body. Do you not know that your body is the temple of the Holy Spirit, who is in you, whom you received from God? You are not your own; you were bought with a price, therefore honor God with your body."

Did you notice the warning in verse 18?

"All other sins a man commits are outside his body, but he who sins sexually, sins against his own body."

Initially, this verse may seem confusing. I can think of all sorts of sins against one's own body; suicide, gluttony, cutting, and drugs just to name a few. So what is God trying to say? The answer becomes apparent when we research the original Greek word for body. When writing here Paul uses the word *soma*. He could have just as easily used the Greek word *sarx*, that actually refers to the fleshly, physical part of us. By choosing *soma* he implies something much deeper. *Soma* means body as in "whole", in the same way that we refer to a "body" of water meaning the water in its entirety. On occasion, someone will refer to an author's "body" of work, and when they do, they are referring to the whole of his literary efforts. This is how Paul uses *soma*; he is telling us that when we sin sexually, we actually sin against our whole person, what you and I would call our personhood. He is warning that sexual sin is different than other sins and when we sin sexually our very personhood is deeply affected.

If you think for a minute this is not true, that sex is just physical... then why is it any different than arm wrestling? Two guys will arm wrestle each other, walk away, and never think twice. But have sex, and you create memories. Suddenly, you're asking the "status" of our relationship. Why... why are we so deeply affected if it is just physical? Isn't it true that some of your deepest regrets center around past sexual behavior? Why? Shaking hands never filled anyone with lifelong regret. Why do we hold in such revulsion someone who molests a child if it is just physical but are less repulsed by someone slapping a child? Slapping is actually physically harmful. Why do we intuitively classify them differently? Because we know in our souls that sexual sin has the capacity to inflict emotional and soulful harm; sexual sin is different from all other sins.

> Because we know in our souls that sexual sin is emotionally and soulfully harmful, sexual sin is different than all other sins.

The uniting principle: vs.15-16 "Do you not know that your bodies are members of Christ himself? Shall I then take the members of Christ and unite them with a prostitute? Never!" Uniting happens during sex because we are spiritual creatures. You and I are different from a dog. A dog has only two parts, a body and a soul. The physical body we see; the soul gives life and personality. But humans are more complex than dogs. We have three parts: body, soul, and spirit. It is this spirit God placed in us that makes us unique from the animals. It is what God was talking about in Genesis 1:26 when after creating the animals He said "Let us make man in our image." That means we are unique from animals. It is this third component to humans that causes us to be self aware, spiritually receptive (you've never seen a dog pray), and is our conscience. Because animals do not possess this spiritual component, they don't respond to life like humans. A lion never thinks to himself after a kill, "I wonder what makes me kill little gazelles? They've never hurt me. I'll bet there is a Mrs. Gazelle and maybe a few gazelle babies. Bet they are missing this guy right about now. I wonder if I should become a vegetarian." The reason a lion never experiences internal conflict is that a lion completely lacks God's gift, the spirit part of humanness.

It is this very spirit that makes sex different for us than animals. This is because our spirit is "sticky." When we engage in sex, it causes us to form attachment/unite with the one we sleep with. It's why immediately after sex, she wants to define the relationship. It is simply a violation of her personhood to give herself to a man and not "unite." Men's spirits are sticky too; men are just far less aware, but the damage of sleeping around and breaking attachment after attachment is still just as profound for a male.

Imagine your spirit is sticky like tape. A girl decides she really does love her first boyfriend, and eventually they sleep together. In that moment, whether she wanted it to or not her spirit attached, remember 1 Corinthians 6:15. Later when she and her boyfriend break up; it's like she peeled the tape of her spirit off carpet and some of the fuzzies came with it. The result is her soul is now less sticky. Next she dates Tom. After six months, their relationship becomes physical. They date for two years then break up, and again the tape of her spirit is pulled away from the carpet of their relationship. This time even more fuzzies come with it. She repeats this pattern throughout college and into adulthood. With each relationship it becomes easier to be physical, and each time the relationship ends, the tape of her spirit is peeled away, and again more fuzzies. This is the problem, just like the tape loses some of its stickiness each time it is peeled away; her spirit also loses some of its stickiness with each relationship that becomes sexual. No wonder we have an epidemic today of couples entering into marriage unable to connect and bond with one another. When hard times come they split rather than fight for their relationship; they simply weren't sticky enough. If this isn't true, and if we don't intuitively understand this principle, why don't men, especially men who are not Christians, seek out prostitutes as highly desirable to marry? If sexual practice with multiple partners makes someone more proficient sexually, then prostitutes should be the most desirable women in our society. They would be able to bring more spice to the bed because of their volume of sexual experience. But that is not how secular or Christian culture views a prostitute. Isn't it because a man knows intuitively that a woman who has lost her stickiness is broken inside?

The One Flesh Principle: God says that when a man and a woman come together physically, something very special happens; they become "one flesh." What is that all about? Simply this; amidst the fun and enjoyment of sex, something much deeper is happening, promises are made, and covenants are promised. Ever wonder why God gave us sex... apart from it being fun... and producing children? God tells us that it was to make us one flesh.

To understand the "one flesh" moment, you have to understand why God gave us

> No wonder we have an epidemic today of couples entering into marriage unable to connect and bond with one another. When hard times come they split rather than fight for their relationship; they simply weren't sticky enough.

baptism. When a person is baptized, they stand in a tank of water and are submerged beneath the water and then raised up again. Baptism is actually a mime where a person acts out what they believe. They are giving a wordless testimony of their faith. Here's how the testimony of baptism works, God knew that many of us, when we came to faith, would not know the words to articulate this new experience in our lives, so He gave us baptism. Without saying a word, when someone stands in the baptismal water, they are declaring that they believe Jesus lived on this earth. When they are "buried" under the water they affirm they believe Jesus actually died for their sins, not passed out, but died. When they are raised out of the water, they are affirming their belief in the resurrection; that Jesus actually and literally came back to life. It's a declaration without words!

Now consider sex, it's a declaration without words! As a man and a woman join their bodies physically as one (kind of like Legos); it is a promise; a covenant play-acted out between a man and a woman, to become one in life. A pledge to face life together, that her problems will be his problems, that his goals will be hers. They become one. That's why when you break off the relationship after having sex, you make yourself a liar; you break the covenant you play acted in bed together! It's the reason marital unfaithfulness is grounds for divorce because the person being unfaithful has broken their one flesh covenant and is entering into a new covenant with someone else.

> Was God being a prude when He said wait, or was He trying to help us experience amazing?

This one flesh principle is why we are not to have sex before marriage, not because God is a killjoy. It's because making that promise over and over again and breaking it over and over again each time your relationship ends cheapens the promise. If someone promises to pay back money they owe you but they have already broken their word by not paying you back the last four times they borrowed money, how hollow do their promises seem now?

Imagine that a couple marries. Both have waited till the honeymoon to have sex. In that night they are declaring their love in an amazing way. They are saying to each other, I love you and only you. Tonight I am entering into a covenant with you to be one flesh, and this promise I am making, I have never made, nor will I ever make, with anyone else! How different is that from the couple who has spent their dating years being sexually active? Now on the honeymoon night what they are miming is, "I am making a promise to you tonight that I have made to nine others. Each one of those people is no longer in my life, and each of my previous promises was broken. But...I want you to trust in tonight, and I want it to mean something special." Was God being a prude when He said wait, or was He trying to help us experience amazing?

The principle of ownership: note vs.19-20

> "Do you not know that your body is the temple of the Holy Spirit, whom you received from God? You are not your own; you were bought with a price. Therefore honor God with your body."

You get that Paul is saying it is unthinkable that a Christian would be promiscuous. This is because no Christian owns their body. The minute you asked Jesus to pay for your sins, you were bought with His blood. The Ownership Certificate of your life left your hands and was passed to God. Because of this, no Christian has the right to give his or her body to anyone else, it's not theirs to give; it belongs to God.

I've never met a Christ follower who said, "my deepest regret is not sleeping around more," but I have met scores of people who wish they had waited for marriage.

141

If I take an Xbox that belongs to my neighbor, and give it to my friend, I'm a thief! So is anyone who takes what belongs to God and gives it to someone else without His permission. If you're a guy, and she's offering herself to you, you're still just as guilty, because you are receiving stolen property. The only time it is ok for a Christian to have sex is inside marriage because God has approved the transfer of property.

Bottom line, you're not a dog, so don't allow some backyard dog to treat you like one. The dog bed is a lie. You can never have sex and it just be physical. Your spirit will go to bed with you and be deeply harmed. The converse is also true; if you wait, something exceptional waits for you. It's what God always hoped for you; to experience "one flesh" with the one you marry in sacred intimacy, and to share something together that neither of you has ever expressed to anyone else. It will be an amazing moment you'll never regret.

Right now, someone is asking, "if you never have sex together, how do you know if they are any good at it." The reality is, none of us were very good at it at first. Waiting doesn't make sex bad; it makes it better. One of the most amazing and fun things in life is a man and a woman discovering each other for the first time. One of the rare joys of newlyweds is to explore and communicate what pleases them physically. Practice makes perfect. My suggestion is once you're married, have tons of practice.

The dog bed is expensive; it lowers your ability to connect intimately with your spouse, and it is filled with regret. I've never met a Christ follower who said, "my deepest regret is not sleeping around more," but I have met scores of people who wish they had waited for marriage.

What if your relationship has already found its way to the dog bed? Here's the good news, God will forgive if you ask Him. Even a guy who loved God like David found himself in the dog bed with Bathsheba. The cool part is that God forgave, and God still used David. But, that's because David repented. So if you're in the dog bed STOP! Make it right with your Heavenly Father. Even though you've slipped up, one day you'll be able to tell your spouse, "Yes, there was a time when I crawled into the dog bed, but when I realized where I was I crawled back out, and from that day forward I have been saving this expression of my love for you." How powerful of a statement would that be?

And if you have any thought of continuing to date the person you're in the dog bed with, I'm going to suggest you need to do some quick assessing as to whether he or she might actually be a backyard dog. If they are, RUN! It's exactly what verse 18 implores you to do "flee youthful lusts." If that's a backyard dog you're in bed with, kick them back out into the backyard and close the door behind them. Even if you decide that the one you're dating is actually an indoor dog, and things have just gotten out of hand, you may still need to end the relationship. Here's why: you've already broken down some fences that should have stayed up. Once you do that, putting those fences back up and remaining sexually pure in a relationship together is almost impossible. That's why often the wisest thing is to end that relationship and date someone with whom you don't have a well-worn path to promiscuity. But if you decide to stay in the relationship, you're going to have to have serious talks right away about setting up new boundaries so that it becomes highly inconvenient to visit the dog bed again. You're going to have to do things that may seem slightly juvenile, like not being out too late alone. You may spend the rest of your dating relationship on group dates and never in rooms alone so that it will be "awkward" to head back to the dog bed again. The rules you decide on need to have enough "teeth" in them that it becomes improbable you'll slip up again. Either way you have lots of talking to do, both with your Heavenly Father and the one you're dating. Go do it now; I'll be here when you get back.

Questions

1. What is the lie the world tells us about sex?

2. How is the Greek word *soma* different from the word *sarx*?

3. The chapter defined three different principles: Uniting, One flesh and Ownership. For you, which of the principles is the strongest argument for abstaining from sex before marriage?

4. Based on what you've learned in this chapter, what will you do?

fifteen

The Big Bed

The reason I call this chapter the big bed is because God actually has big plans for your sex life! He's hoping you will have amazing, earth shattering, over the moon sex. That's what He has always hoped for you, and He is not nearly as hung up about sex as you may think He is. After all, He's the one who created and designed the plumbing. He's not in heaven right now nudging Gabriel and saying, "do you see what they're doing down there? I never imagined they'd use it for that!" Just the opposite, God created sex for men and women to enjoy one another. If you doubt that, you haven't read your Bible lately:

> "Then God created man in his own image, in the image of God he created him; male and female he created them. God blessed them and said to them, 'Be fruitful and increase in number...'" Genesis 1:27-28

Any guesses as to how they were going to accomplish being fruitful and multiplying? Have you ever considered that God's first command recorded in scripture was to have sex?

> "The Lord said, 'It is not good for man to be alone.'" Genesis 2:15

God could have made another man for Adam to hang out with and play video games; instead He reverse engineered the plumbing.

> "For this reason a man will leave his father and mother and be united to his wife, and they shall become one flesh." Genesis 2:24

The sign that they were establishing their own home was sex.

> "The man and his wife were both naked, and they" felt no shame." Genesis 2:25

NAKED! How convenient was that? Everything was readily accessible. You realize God started us off as a nudist colony, and we blew that one!

> "Adam lay with his wife Eve, and she became pregnant..." Genesis 4:1

If you're reading the Bible, that's just the first thirty minutes! Right about now the men reading this are thinking "I need to read my Bible a lot more", and you're right.

There is an entire book of the Bible written about sex (Song of Solomon). There are all sorts of sexcapades in the Bible: Onan and his brother's wife, David and Bathsheba, Amnon and Tamar, Absalom and his father's concubines, Solomon and his seven hundred wives and three hundred concubines (who would have the time and how would you keep their names straight?), and Sampson and Delilah. Sex in the Bible would be worthy of multiple episodes of the *Jerry Springer Show.*

God even commands husbands and wives not to stop having sex:

> "The husband should fulfill his marital duty to his wife (sex), and likewise the wife to her husband (sex). The wife's body does not belong to her alone but also to her husband. In the same way, the husband's body does not belong to him alone but also to his wife. Do not deprive each other (of sex) except by mutual consent and for a time, so that you may devote yourselves to prayer. Then come together again (for sex) so that Satan will not tempt you because of your lack of self control" 1 Corinthians 7:3-5

Hopefully, I haven't embarrassed everyone to the point of closing this book and never opening it again. The idea is simply this: God is not freaked out by sex. He created it for us to enjoy. The problem is we took what was meant to be life's most beautiful and selfless expression between a man and woman and really messed it up! Instead of sex being about a husband and wife putting each other first and doing everything they could to fulfill one another, sex has been twisted into individuals saying and doing whatever is necessary to get what they want from one another. We have turned sex into something deeply selfish and disappointing.

This is where the big bed comes in. It's time for Christians to reclaim the wonder of sex. If sex is God's gift then God followers should be the best at it. So what did God hope we would do with sex when He created it?

The one flesh promise: We've already touched on this. God's desire was that the coming together of a man and woman sexually would express a promise between them that no one else on this earth shared. This is the essence of when sex truly becomes lovemaking. It is in this moment a man and a woman express to each other an intimacy that they share with no other human. When their two bodies come together to form one, it is the promise to be one. It is an expression of love so important that there is to be only one person in the world they give it to. Because it was reserved for marriage, the gift becomes that much more sacred.

It is a promise between a man and woman that the oneness they are experiencing together in the marital bed will be equally expressed in the oneness they live out the rest of their marriage.

The submitting to one another principle: In Ephesians 5:21 as Paul begins to give instruction on marriage his first admonition is "Submit to one another out of reverence for Christ." Big bed sex is the opportunity to practice putting the needs of the other person above our own. It should be every man's priority in sex to make sure his wife is having an amazing experience. His greatest excitement should come from her pleasure. Not only is this a lot of fun, but also it makes it much more likely she will be thrilled at the prospect of being with him again. Men who have wives who lay still like mannequins enduring sex have not mastered this selfless act of putting her needs above his. In the same way the wife is to actively seek to please her man. She is to do all she can to make the moment thrilling by making his needs her priority. Think for a moment how fun that kind of sex can be. Two people focused on physically pleasing the other. This is exactly what God designed us for, the unselfish expression of love between a man and a woman.

> All those moments become easier because we've practiced putting the other first.

That kind of lovemaking actually becomes practice for putting our spouse first in every other encounter of our marriage. It's how we are to behave when we choose where to go for dinner, or who will get a break from the kids tonight, or how we will resolve disagreements. All those moments become easier because we've practiced putting the other first in the marriage bed.

Pour on top of all that the sheer fun of sex, and you have big bed sex the way God intended! It also underlines why the selfishness of the dog bed is doomed to disappoint and is such a violent insult to God's gift of sex. Imagine that I give you a gift, a violin. Upon examination you notice it's dusty has some scratches, and the strings are well worn. It's pretty obvious it is old and has seen better days. You toss it into the back of your closest. Over the years suitcases are stacked on it. It gets bumped as you move it around, and after several years, you give it to Goodwill. One day I inquire, "Where's the violin I gave you?" You explain that you held onto it for a while, but eventually it was just wasting space.

In shock I explain to you that the violin was a Stradivarius hand created by Antonio Stradivari himself. That at one time Napoleon Bonaparte owned it, and that the sound that violin was capable of producing, no other type of violin in the world could produce the same magical sound. In frustration, you ask, "Why didn't you tell me how valuable it was, I would have treated it differently, I would have treasured it."

Now that you know just how valuable and sacred this gift of sex is, shouldn't you treat it differently than your friends who have no idea of its true value, and whatever you do, never take it to the dog bed?

Questions

1. God created sex. How does that change your view of sex?

2. When does sex become lovemaking?

3. What does submitting to each other's needs teach us about the rest of married life?

4. What's the most significant thing you picked up in this chapter?

Dating an Indoor Dog

sixteen

Establishing Sexual Limits

Hopefully you've already come to the conclusion that sex before marriage is a big deal. Sex with someone causes you to bond with him or her in a way that can cloud objective thinking about the relationship. Later, when unhealthy habits and red flags emerge, sexually active people tend to overlook them because they already feel an intense bond. If you're trying to trap someone in a relationship, sex may be your weapon of choice, but if you're truly looking for God's best, sex before marriage will only get in the way. It will create a temporary loyalty that will rival God and cloud your mind. It will place you out of fellowship with God making hearing His voice almost impossible. This would be absolutely foolish if you were hoping God would help direct you to the right one!

My encouragement is that very early in the process of dating someone you talk through sexual limits. I know that sex can be an awkward conversation; so, I'll give you permission to wait till the second date. If the person you're dating attempts something inappropriate on the first date, you already have your answer, and no discussion is needed since there shouldn't be a second date.

Both of you should commit to hold the other accountable. In all likelihood, at any given moment one of you will be weaker and the other will be stronger. We'll talk about how to handle this moment in the next chapter. For now, here are some proposed limits to be discussed:

(1) **Be Careful Little Hands:** If it's inappropriate for a cousin to touch you there, then it is inappropriate for the person you're dating to touch you there. Scripture in discussing the church and its many parts uses the example of the parts of our physical bodies that require modesty and special honor.

> "On the contrary, those parts of the body that seem to be weaker are indispensable, and the parts that we think are less honorable *we treat with special honor*_(emphasis mine). And the parts that are unpresentable are treated with special modesty, while our presentable parts need no special treatment." 1 Corinthians 12:22-24a

Clearly there are parts of our body that are to be honored and access limited until we are married. Paul says:

> "Do you not know that your body is a temple of the Holy Spirit, who is in you, whom you received from God? You are not your own, you were bought with a price. Therefore honor God with your body." 1 Corinthians 6:19-20

Paul clearly says that your body is not yours to give. If you give yourself to someone who is not your spouse and they sleep with you, you are both thieves. You've taken what belongs to God without permission. Another interesting aspect of the passage is that Paul reminds us the Holy Spirit lives in us. That means the Holy Spirit, God Himself, is present when we have sex.

When I was a young intern at a church in Arizona, I still lived at home with my mom. She is one of the godliest women I know. My wife Lisa often refers to her as Jesus in a dress. One day I invited her to watch a movie with me I had rented. She was not initially interested, but I assured her that I had already seen the movie, and it was amazing. Probably one of the funniest movies I had ever seen. After much cajoling, she finally relented to watch with me.

Unfortunately, I had forgotten the rampant cursing and use of the Lord's name in the movie. It was filled with sexual innuendo. Sitting there with my saintly mom quickly became mortifyingly uncomfortable. After what seemed like an eternity, probably less than ten minutes, she excused herself to go do some housework. I sat there in embarrassment; not only had I subjected my mom to a crude unsavory movie, but I had also assured her that I had watched it already and had given it my endorsement. Hearing those words and coarse jokes in the presence of my mom made their darkness so much more vivid. It was like someone turned on a light, and suddenly I saw the real ugliness in the movie.

> Because the Holy Spirit lives in us, He is present for whatever sexual encounter we have.

Because the Holy Spirit lives in us, He is present for

whatever sexual encounter we have. God is right there watching...observing. It would be weird enough if your parents were watching you have sex, but God?

There's a story I heard years ago about a couple, we'll call them Jeff and Cindy. They were both Christians and had recently become engaged. Tuesday night was the two-year anniversary of their first date. Cindy's mom and dad were going to be out of town on vacation, and Cindy asked if she could have Jeff over and cook dinner for him. At first mom was hesitant; it didn't seem wise for them to be alone together in the house. Finally, she relented. Jeff and Cindy had been dating all this time and had been waiting to have sex for marriage. Mom and Dad decided they could be trusted.

The night came for the special dinner. Jeff showed up looking better than ever. Cindy had taken extra time to look exceptional for him. As they ate, it was almost a foreshadowing of what being married would look like. There was tons of animal attraction in the air. Eventually, Jeff said in a quiet whisper, "I can't wait any longer." Cindy knew exactly what he meant. Truth was, Cindy was feeling the same way. They leapt up from the table and ended up in Cindy's parent's bedroom. Clothes were flying, and things were just beginning to progress when the phone rang.

Cindy looked at Jeff who said, "don't answer it." "I have to, it may be my parents, and they'll be suspicious if we don't pick up," replied Cindy. Sure enough, it was Dad. Dad explained that when they left he forgot to turn off the pilot light on the furnace. It had been acting up, and he was very concerned that it might be dangerous. He made her swear she would immediately go down to the basement and turn off the pilot on the heater.

Hanging up the phone, she explained her conversation she had with her dad to Jeff and what she needed to do, and told him she would be right back. Jeff was fearful that if she went alone, she might lose the passion of the moment. So, wanting to keep the romance burning, he scooped up Cindy and began to carry her down to the basement, both of them completely naked. When they got to the bottom of the stairs Jeff heroically kicked the door open, and stepped into the basement to shouts of "Surprise." Turned out Mom and Dad had planned an engagement party. Jeff immediately dropped Cindy to the floor and ran. Standing in the room dumbfounded were all their friends... worse yet Mom and Dad...even worse... their pastor...and if that weren't bad enough...Grandma was there! If that's embarrassing, how much more embarrassing should it be for a Christian couple to have premarital sex in front of their Heavenly Father? Think about that the next time things get a little heavy on the couch. It might just change the mood.

(2) **Keep It Warm, Just Not Hot:** You should never defraud the person you are dating.

> "It is God's will that you should be sanctified;
> that you should avoid sexual immorality; that
> each of you should learn to control his own
> body in a way that is holy and honorable, not
> in passionate lust like the heathen, who do
> not know God; and that in this matter no one

should wrong his brother or take advantage of him. The Lord will punish men for all such sins…" 1 Thessalonians 4:3-6a

Note the word here translated "wrong" in the NIV is translated more accurately in the KJV as "defraud." To defraud is to promise someone something you can't fulfill. It's a legal term that would be used if someone sold you a bridge; only to find out they really didn't own it and had no right to give it to you. Sound familiar? This is especially important to understand because a lot of Christians in an effort to not have intercourse instead try to see how turned on they can make one another without removing their clothes. The problem is, you're causing your date to majorly lust. What may seem like a game is serious sin. You're defrauding them, causing them to desire, and I would argue you are promising them something with your actions you cannot righteously fulfill. Turning on the person you're with simply for the rush of it, or the ego strokes that come with knowing they are attracted to you and you can get them all hot and bothered, is extremely cruel and not Christ-like.

The standard for what's appropriate for a couple are actually pretty simple. If modesty requires she cover it, you have no business touching it. That part of her body belongs to the Lord until it is given as His gift to her spouse in marriage. On the contrary, rather than exploit and manipulate a woman's love for him, a man is to protect her heart and her soul. He is to hold them in sacred trust until the day she can honorably give herself to him.

"Jesus said, 'But I tell you that anyone who looks at a woman lustfully has already committed adultery with her in his heart.'"
Matthew 5:28

When you're in a heavy make out session and things get overly heated, you've gone way beyond looking and lusting. Don't get me wrong, I'm all for a little making out. I like kissing. I like kissing a lot. Maybe even more than the next guy, but you and I are commanded to be careful and not cross the line into lusting, or causing the person you're with to lust.

I once knew a gal who thought it was ok to let her boyfriend touch her breasts. Her rational was that it did nothing for her, nothing about it excited her or caused her to lust, hence she wasn't sinning. But scripture here is teaching something much more profound, it is saying that I am my brother's keeper. That I have an obligation to not be a stumbling block for someone else, to not cause them to desire something, which we cannot righteously have.

You need to know that if you are willingly causing the person you're with to lust, you are teaching them to be a proficient luster. After all, practice makes perfect. You are sending them a clear message that messing around with someone outside the bonds of marriage is acceptable in your world. So, let's say you actually do get married, please don't tell me you expect them to be faithful to you. Why? Everything you've taught and reinforced throughout your time dating is how to be an accomplished luster. You've clearly reinforced that it's ok to derive sexual pleasure from someone you are not married to. You've trained up your own backyard dog. Now, you want them to ignore your training and become a non-lusting indoor dog? Good luck with that!

You may be asking, how much making out is too much making out? How do you know when it is time to slow things down? Interestingly enough, God has equipped the male of the species with a warning device. The truth is, every male knows when he's getting excited. I'm convinced God intended this as a gift. If you are sensing a strong response, it's time for you to take immediate corrective action. Need I say more?

(3) Respect What You Borrow: Chances are you're dating someone else's future spouse. Most of us will date multiple people before we find the one. I know you think the one you're dating is the one, but maybe not. They may be someone else's one. Only go as far as you're willing for your future spouse to be going on their date. This one gets a little iffy because culture has so seared our morals. Many would say, "I don't expect my future spouse to be a virgin." We seem to have more regard for our I-pad than we do our future mate. We would be infuriated if someone took and abused our I-pad, scratching the screen, downloading random apps, deleting others, and changing our settings. Yet when it comes to our spouse they are free to put their hands all over them, create lifelong regret, impair their ability to connect emotionally with us, jeopardize their relationship with God, and we don't seem to care. Here's a thought; treat the one you're dating like they are borrowed, because they are. Whether borrowed from God, because you're not married yet, or borrowed from their future spouse, you're borrowing.

My policy is that if I borrow someone's car I want to leave it better than I found it. I always return it with a full tank even if the tank was empty when I took it, and I didn't drive it very far. Often I'll take the car to be washed before I return it. I do this because it's a matter of honor. I want the person who loaned me the car to know that anything they place in my hands will be treated with better care than I would treat my own stuff.

> Wouldn't it be exciting if God brought you several people to date, not because you were going to marry them, but because dating you would be the time of their greatest growth in Christ?

How cool would it be if you made yourself and God a promise that anyone He trusts you to date will be better for having dated you? That would make you an indoor dog for sure! Wouldn't it be exciting if God brought you several people to date, not because you were going to marry them, but because dating you would be the time of their greatest growth in Christ? What if one day, their spouse would say to you, "Thanks for dating my wife/husband, you were probably the greatest blessing in their life, and the person God used to prepare them for me. They are way better for having dated you." Shouldn't that be our goal in dating? That everyone we date ends up closer to God for having dated us?

Questions

1. Why is it important to establish sexual limits?

2. What is the danger in having sex before marriage?

3. Who actually owns your body?

4. Thinking about Jeff and Cindy, why should the fact that God is with you cause you to reconsider sex before marriage?

5. How do people cause others to lust? Why is causing your date to lust an issue?

6. What should be the goal for each of your dating relationships?

seventeen

Pulling a Joseph

No matter how vigilant you are chances are sometime while you're dating things are going to begin to get a little too hot and heavy. Thoughts will be racing through your mind. Hormones will be pleading for satisfaction. You will find yourself facing a decision to either take things to the next level or to find a way to cool off.

Scripture provides us a model for what to do next:

> "Now Joseph was well built and handsome, and after a while his master's wife took notice of Joseph and said, "Come to bed with me!" But he refused. "With me in charge," he told her, "my master does not concern himself with anything in the house; everything he owns he has entrusted to my care. No one is greater in this house than I am. My master has withheld nothing from me except you, because you are his wife. How then could I do such a wicked thing and sin against God?" And though she spoke to Joseph day and night, he refused to go to bed with her or even be with her. One day he went into the house to attend to his duties, and none of the household servants was inside. She caught him by his cloak and said, "Come to bed with

me." But he left the cloak in her hand and ran
from the house." Genesis 39:6b-12

Note, Joseph understood that sleeping with Potiphar's
wife would not only be a sin against Potiphar, but also
against God. He actually could have come up with some
pretty good excuses to indulge his desires; "God allowed me
to be sold into slavery by my brothers." "This woman has
authority over me; maybe I should obey her". "Not giving
in to her could get me into a whole bunch more trouble."
He could have easily justified sin. You and I have our own
set of excuses, "everyone else is doing it. We are going to
get married. We really do love each other". Excuses are
just that, excuses. They do not change the fact that wrong
is wrong, and sin is sin. Joseph didn't let excuses trump
character.

I actually believe Joseph was tempted big time. Here's
why, if Potiphar's wife were as ugly as a mud fence, or if her
breath smelled like raw sewage, Joseph would have laughed
at her advances, or calmly explained why he couldn't...
shouldn't sleep with her. If he wasn't attracted, he would
have said, "not on your luckiest day and my worst is it going
to happen." Instead when she keeps pressing the issue,
he flees! I'm convinced he's sweating bullets of lust. If he
stays there one minute more he's going do something he
will regret, so he screams out loud and runs as far from
temptation as he can.

My advice for you is to do the same. Try it! Next time
you're in a make out session and things get too hot and
heavy, and you're about to go too far, scream. Scream as

loud as you can and then run from the room all the while waving your arms. Here's what I promise, you'll break the mood. I guarantee things will cool off pronto. Second, the person you were with will be much slower to push the limit again for fear of a repeat performance.

Ok, so maybe that's not the most practical idea, but the principle is the same. Run! When you find yourself being tempted to a point that doing what you shouldn't do actually begins to look like what you need to do; run. 1 Corinthians 6:18 says the same thing:

"Flee sexual immorality."

Running may mean that you have to right then and there discuss and establish new guidelines for how much time you'll spend alone and in what context. Doors to rooms probably need to remain open and double dates may be in order for the rest of your dating relationship. Fleeing means that what just almost happened cannot happen again. You need to run away from that danger and create a real buffer.

In contrast, stay in that moment, be foolish enough to believe you can flirt with that line and not get burned, and you will eventually go where you promised you would never go. You'll forever change the nature of your relationship when you turn your relationship pyramid upside down. Believe me, I know. While I was still in Bible College I started dating someone from the church's single's group. She was an indoor dog. She loved the Lord and served in leadership in the group. She served tirelessly in ministry. We began dating, and I thought I might have found "The

One". Even though we worked to keep God in the center of the relationship, going to Bible studies and serving together, we kept progressing further and further physically. One night my hands went where they shouldn't. We hadn't gone all the way, but we had touched things we had no business touching. We immediately confessed and promised God and ourselves it would never happen again. Unfortunately, we didn't create any buffer. We continued to be alone and do a lot of heavy making out. Inevitably we would go too far. Over and over again we would pray and confess, and promise each other and the Lord we would never cross those lines again. The problem was, we had already torn down the fences between where we belonged and where we shouldn't go. The path was already worn, and each time we were together the memories of those lustful moments were front and center. I already knew what was underneath those clothes, and that knowledge made holding back impossible. We couldn't keep on like we were; we were hurting each other and our relationship with God. I knew our disobedience had brought us to a crossroad. Scripture says:

> "Now to the unmarried and widows I say: It is good for them to stay unmarried, as I am. But if they cannot control themselves, they should marry, for it is better to marry than to burn with passion...If anyone thinks he is acting improperly toward the virgin he is engaged to, and if she is getting along in years and he feels he ought to marry, he should do

as he wants, he is not sinning." 1 Corinthians
7:8-9, 36

I knew I either needed to marry her or break up. After a
lot of prayer and soul searching I knew I was not ready to
make a life long commitment to her.
She was heartbroken. I'm sure one of
the justifications of her heart as we
became physical was that she fully
expected to marry me. I knew we
were in trouble headed for more
trouble. Because I couldn't trust
myself, it actually cut the length of
our courtship short.

> Ironically, it's
> the outdoor
> dog that
> stays after
> it becomes
> physical.

When indoor dogs feel convicted they respond to the
conviction. In this case because I was an indoor dog, I pulled
a Joseph; I fled from the unhealthy relationship. Every
woman should take note of his truth. If you're dating an
indoor dog and you allow the relationship to get physical,
you may actually lose the relationship. If he is truly an
indoor dog, he will hate the feeling of conviction. If he's
not ready to put a ring on your finger immediately, he may
be compelled to break off the relationship. Ironically, it's
the outdoor dog that stays after it becomes physical. Since
the outdoor dog either doesn't know God or is backslidden,
conviction is not a big thing to him, and he is more than
happy to keep pursuing you physically even at the expense
of yours and his relationship with God.

Bottom line, if your physical relationship is creeping up
on the limits of what's Biblical, right now may be a great

time for a discussion. Talk about steps you are going to take to keep from going too far. Make wise choices about whether you'll be alone together and under what circumstances. Will others be in close proximity with doors open? This will make getting too physical unlikely. If you've already gone too far, and you want to try to continue dating, you will need to double date for the rest of your courtship. If you can't keep your hands off of each other, it may be time to flee. Pull a Joseph...and no matter how attracted you are, or how much you may love the other person, love God more. If you're not ready to marry, don't continue to burn with lust, leave the relationship. It may be the hardest thing you ever do, but it will make your Heavenly Father proud, and maybe your earthly one too.

> Pull a Joseph...
> and no matter
> how attracted
> you are, or
> how much you
> may love the
> other person,
> love God more.

Questions

1. Why did Joseph refuse to sleep with Potiphar's wife?

2. What are some excuses Joseph could have used to justify sleeping with her?

3. What are some of the excuses people use to justify sex before marriage?

4. Once a couple has gone too far, why is it so hard not to go there again?

5. What are some crazy ways you can flee from sexual immorality?

eighteen

The Non-Negotiables

Earlier in this book I told you the story of the youth pastor who challenged my wife Lisa to list her five non-negotiables for a future mate. I told you that God reserved two for Himself, but the other three were entirely up to you. So lets get to work on our list. We are going to assume that whomever you marry is attractive to you. You don't even need to put that on the list. If they don't get your heart racing, don't bother. The two areas God reserves for Himself are that they must be a believer, and they need to be a matched set with you, meaning they need to be somewhere in proximity to your present spiritual maturity. God made both of these stipulations because He loves you and wants the very best for you.

Churches are full of miss-matched couples, believers who married non-believers, and Christians who married way below their own maturity level. I have never heard any one of these couples in hind site say, if they could do it over again, they would do the same thing. That's not to say they don't love their spouse; it's just that marriage has been way harder than it needed to be if they had heeded God. How cautionary is that to your heart; that those who have gone before you and made the mistake of ignoring God's prescription almost always acknowledge that it was a mistake later? Even those whose spouses later accepted Christ, or grew by leaps and bounds affirm they dodged a bullet. I've never heard one of those couples say it wasn't a big deal or that they would advise anyone else to repeat their mistake. Most of the time these couples are the first to beg others not to follow in their footsteps. Believe me, I have spent countless hours with couples working through the pain caused by ignoring God's commands for dating. The reality is that for most, I had to tell them they were stuck with their decision and needed to try and make the best of a bad situation.

So, let's assume you're convinced. You want only an indoor dog, and no outdoor dogs need apply. You've determined you are looking for a Christian who is comparable in the depth of their maturity. You are committing yourself to keep God's non-negotiables as your first two non-negotiables. I believe there are some other values that deserve some consideration as you fill in your final three.

No authority issues: People who struggle with authority are doomed to a lifetime of contention. If someone consistently struggles with those in authority over them, they will struggle with God. If they resist directives from someone they can hear audibly and who is paying them to listen (their boss), how much more do you expect they'll struggle with following a God who speaks in a still small voice and asks them to do highly difficult and unpopular things? If a young man refuses to listen to his parents, how carefully do you suppose he'll listen to God as he leads his home? Date a young lady who doesn't honor her father, wait till you're her husband and lead in a way she doesn't agree with. Bottom line; invite someone into your life with authority issues and you're inviting a lifetime of arguments.

Terri started dating Todd in College. Despite the fact that several friends had conversations with her about Todd, she continued to date him. Friends were concerned that he seemed angry and stubborn. Terri was sure he had just endured a lot of unfairness in his life and needed someone to love him. Eventually they were married. Todd went into ministry as a youth pastor in a growing church. Even though this was Todd's first ministry job and the Senior Pastor had nearly two decades of experience, Todd was convinced he knew more about running the church than the pastor. Eventually, Todd became so frustrated that his ideas were not being implemented he told off the senior pastor and resigned.

Todd got a second youth pastorate in a church in California. Within 24 months he was again frustrated the staff that had a combined 40+ years of experience were not responding to the major adjustments he was proposing. Eventually, Todd decided that church in general was too messed up, and he left ministry.

He then started a job in construction, but he constantly critiqued and criticized the company's owner. Even though this was a new field for him, he was sure the owner was making multiple mistakes. Todd decided to apply for the job he had always wanted, so he interviewed to be a police officer. A little ironic since Todd didn't want to take orders from anyone, now he wanted to be the one giving the orders. There was something in Todd's past that caused multiple departments to turn Todd down. All the while,

Terri had to endure the ups and downs of Todd's career path. Constantly living with inconsistent income because of the frequent times Todd would quit a job because his boss was "incompetent" or he had been released for being insubordinate. Along the way they had four children, and Terri would do her best to keep the children's spirits high all the while pleading for patience for their dad.

Finally, Todd was offered a job in a public service role, and you've guessed it...within weeks he was complaining about his supervisor. Eventually Todd resolved to stick with it. So now, his discontent turned a new direction, toward Terri. Eventually after having multiple affairs and Terri taking him back each time, he announced she no longer made him happy, and he was leaving.

When his pastor met with Todd, he pleaded with him to reconsider. The pastor pointed out that leaving his wife and children was direct disobedience to God, that no one can disobey God and end up happy. He cautioned Todd that his decision would bring unimaginable pain to his children. How many guesses do you need about what he did next? He left. He left because he was smarter than every boss he had ever had, smarter than his pastor, and smarter than God. Needless to say, Todd has authority issues. Terri's biggest mistake was being willing to date a man who struggled with authority.

> "A man who remains stiff-necked after many rebukes will suddenly be destroyed – without remedy." Proverbs 29:1

The Good Fighter: In your relationship, there will be disagreements. There is almost nothing that can bring more chaos into your life than someone who fights to win an argument instead of fighting for the relationship. Fighting for the relationship means not actually fighting at all. It's holding emotions in check and refusing to call names or play the blame game. It means focusing on solutions and changing behaviors and goals so that the current problem will not be a problem again.

Lisa and I are working on 33 years of marriage. We are both first born and natural born leaders. We have all the potential in the world to have world-class fights. Yet we've had almost none. Early on, Lisa and I chose not to fight to win. With our strong personalities, something would have ended up broken. We decided instead to fight/work for a solution so that whatever had caused us so much angst in the first place would never be an issue again.

Believe me, over the years, I've had moments of real frustration with Lisa. There have been moments when trading her in looked like a legitimate option. Then I remembered we had committed to each other for life before God. Since neither of us was going anywhere, I knew I didn't want to spend the next forty years having this same argument over and over again. So? We got together and agreed to a solution. We set up rules for how we would navigate that same situation the next time it came up. At this point, I don't think either of us would ever consider leaving the other for someone else; we have too much work invested in each other. If that doesn't sound loving to you, let me assure you it is, it was love that stilled our tongues when we wanted to attack. It was love that kept us up late hashing out respectful answers to our disagreements. And, it is love that causes us to honor the agreements we've worked out together.

So, as you date, what happens when you disagree? Do hurtful words get used as weapons? Is admitting they were wrong an impossibility? Does anger cloud clear discussion? If you had a disagreement in public, would someone observing you conclude that you must be Christians based on the honor and respect you afford one another? The old saying: "sticks and stones may break my bones but words will never hurt me" is a lie. Words cause wounds that may never heal. If someone fights dirty when you're dating, you can be sure they'll bring out the big guns once you say I do. Save yourself a lot of pain. Find someone who even when they disagree treats you with honor and respect, someone who chooses to keep his or her anger at bay. Most of all, find someone who works for a solution so that the relationship is actually stronger after a disagreement.

Here's the really cool part, the last three are really up to you. God gave you lots of freedom to find someone who thrills your heart. Is a good sense of humor a big deal? Maybe being wise with money is your priority. You can opt for a foreign accent or red hair. God's cool with it. He wants you to be thrilled with the one who makes your list.

> The winner is not the one who dates the most; it's the one who dates the best.

Do yourself a favor from this day forward, have the courage to turn away anyone who doesn't meet your top five. Don't compromise! Stick to your guns. You probably will date less, may watch some really cute people walk away. But, you only need one indoor dog. The winner is not the one who dates the most; it's the one who dates the best.

Questions

1. What are God's two non-negotiables?

2. Why are authority issues a big deal for the person you date?

3. What does "fighting fair" look like?

4. What's the difference between fighting to win and working for a solution?

5. Now is the time to head to the back of this book and fill out your non-negotiables. Give God His first two.

nineteen

Nine-Dollar Light Bulbs

Today I bought a nine-dollar light bulb. The irony is, the nine-dollar light bulb was right next to several three-dollar light bulbs. You may think I'm crazy but before you make a final decision, hear me out. I was buying the bulb to go into a fixture in my 12' ceiling on an upper planter shelf above a fireplace. My ceilings are rather high, and every time this bulb goes out it usually takes me several months before I actually find enough resolve to replace it. That's because the large ladder I need to use is so bulky, and once I'm at the top, the bulb is located in a really awkward spot. To reach it, I have to lean back and twist my arm behind my head.

The new bulb I was choosing to purchase was guaranteed for twenty-two years. That means by the time it wears out, I'll be too old to replace it. I'll send my grandson to do it. Besides, I was replacing the three-dollar bulbs about every two years, that means in six years I'm even. By the time the bulb burns out, it will actually save me twenty- four dollars. On top of that the new bulb is a LED, and it uses far less electricity. The package said it would save me another three hundred and twenty four dollars over the life of the bulb. So, in the end I never replace that bulb again and save three hundred forty eight dollars. In the future when I listen to my neighbors complain about replacing their fireplace bulb every two years, and all the cost and trouble that one bulb has caused, I'll smile and be very thankful for my nine-dollar bulb.

That's how marriage is. Right now, you can take the cheap route. You can date your three-dollar bulb/backyard dog and save a little money/effort in the short term. Backyard dogs are convenient, they are a dime a dozen, and there are plenty to go around. Or, you can pay a little more now to save big time in the future. Hopefully, you will resolve to turn down dates from backyard dogs. Move on as soon as you realize they don't meet the non-negotiables. If you do, one day when your friends are complaining about the backyard dog they married, how they poop and pee in the house, chew up the furniture, fight unfairly, flirt with their secretary, gamble the household money away, or stay up late watching porn ... you can smile. You'll be thrilled you took the time and had the courage to date only indoor dogs. I know. I'm glad I did.

My Non-Negotiables

1. _____

2. _____

3. _____

4. _____

5. _____